2015 FAIR ♥ ISLE COLLECTION

by Knit Picks

Printed in the United States of America

Second Printing, 2015

ISBN 978-1-62767-065-4

Versa Press, Inc
800-447-7829

www.versapress.com

CONTENTS

INTRODUCTION

Fair Isle is a technique long loved by knitters who enjoy stranding yarn to create dramatic, colorful results. Steeped in tradition yet also used in modern, stunning garments, this technique is one every knitter is tempted to try. Heads will turn at the sight of these garments, and jaws will drop open when admirers understand that you've made these gorgeous items yourself.

The 2015 Knit Picks Fair Isle Collection contains patterns for novices and fair isle experts alike. Start with simple sachets and graduate to steeked pullovers in a master class of patterns that will challenge and delight you. Visit our fair isle and colorwork tutorials at knitpicks.com/fairisletutorials for how-tos on stranded knitting, steeking, and choosing colors.

From pillows and cardigans to mittens and hats, we hope you'll return to this pattern collection time and time again, whenever the desire to do colorwork strikes. Choose your color palate and get started on your knitting journey to the Shetland Isles, without ever leaving your favorite chair! These projects are sure to take you to lofty places.

FAIR ISLE LAVENDER SACHETS

by Anna Davis

FINISHED MEASUREMENTS

Turkish Delight 5.5 x 5"; Chevrons 5.5 x 5"; Crusader 5.5 x 5.25"; Highlander 5.5 x 4.75"

YARN

Knit Picks Palette Fingering Weight (100% Peruvian Highland Wool; 231 yards/50g): MC Cream 23730, 1 ball; C1 Canary 25531 1 ball; C2 Caribbean 25095 1 ball; C3 Regal 25089 1 ball; C4 Rouge 24567, 1 ball

NEEDLES

US 3 (3.25mm) straight needles, or size to obtain gauge

US 3 (3.25mm) DPNs, or same size as to obtain gauge

NOTIONS

Yarn Needle

Dried Lavender Buds

GAUGE

28 sts and 32 rows = 4" in stranded Stockinette st, blocked.

Fair Isle Lavender Sachets

Notes:
Each lavender sachet is knit flat in stranded Stockinette stitch, worked in three colors and features its own individual charted Fair Isle pattern. Charts are read from the bottom up, from right to left for RS (even numbered) rows, and from left to right for WS (odd numbered) rows. Each chart begins on a WS (purled) row. Each charted pattern has the same background color, which is considered the Main Color. The Contrast Color changes occur every two rows on the RS only, and are carried up the side on the wrong side of piece. While stranding, the MC is carried across the wrong side and stranded over the top of the CC strand. This helps maintain consistent color dominance and yarn tensions between all four sachets. A separate I-cord trim is sewn around the edges after blocking, seaming, and stuffing each sachet.

Stockinette Stitch (worked flat)
Row 1 (WS): Purl.
Row 2 (RS): Knit.
Repeat Rows 1 and 2 for pattern.

DIRECTIONS

Turkish Delight

Front
With MC, CO 39 sts. Begin Chart 1: Turkish Delight.
Row 1 (WS): Purl to end.
Rows 2-40: Following chart, work in stranded Stockinette st, working all even numbered rows in Knit sts, and all odd numbered rows in Purl sts.
Next Row (WS): Loosely BO all sts purlwise using MC.

Back
Repeat directions as given for Front.

Chevrons

Front
With MC, CO 38 sts. Begin Chart 2: Chevrons.
Row 1 (WS): Purl to end.
Rows 2-40: Following chart, work in stranded Stockinette st, working all even numbered rows in Knit sts, and all odd numbered rows in Purl sts
Next Row (WS): Loosely BO all sts purlwise using MC.

Back
Repeat directions as given for Front.

Crusader

Front
With MC, CO 39 sts. Begin Chart 3: Crusader.
Row 1 (WS): Purl to end.
Rows 2-42: Following chart, work in stranded Stockinette st, working all even numbered rows in Knit sts, and all odd numbered rows in Purl sts
Next Row (WS): Loosely BO all sts purlwise using MC.

Back
Repeat directions as given for Front.

Highlander

Front
With MC, CO 39 sts. Begin Chart 4: Highlander.
Row 1 (WS): Purl to end.
Rows 2-38: Work in stranded Stockinette st, working all even numbered rows in Knit sts, and all odd numbered rows in Purl sts
Next Row (WS): Loosely BO all sts purlwise using MC.

Back
Repeat directions as given for Front.

I-cord Trim

Note: I-cord stretches lengthwise, therefore lengths given are approximate. I-cord length can be easily adjusted by working to a longer length than desired, un-knotting the end, and ripping out excess rows.

Using US 3 (3.25mm) dpns, and with MC, CO 3 sts. *Knit across row. Do not turn work. Slide sts to other end of needle, pull working yarn firmly*. Rep from * to *, creating a tube. Work to the following lengths: Turkish Delight: 22", Chevrons: 22", Crusader: 22.5", Highlander 21.5". Leaving a long tail for sewing the I-cord to the lavender sachet edges, break yarn. With RS facing use yarn needle to thread through every stitch of final row and pull gently to close I-cord at top.

Finishing

Weave in ends. Prior to seaming, wet and block to finished measurements. With MC, sew top and side seams, leaving bottom seam open. Insert dried lavender buds. Do not over-fill. Sew bottom seam. With MC, sew I-cord trim around edges.

Turkish Delight Chart

Legend

- MC
- C1
- C2
- C3
- C4

Chevrons Chart

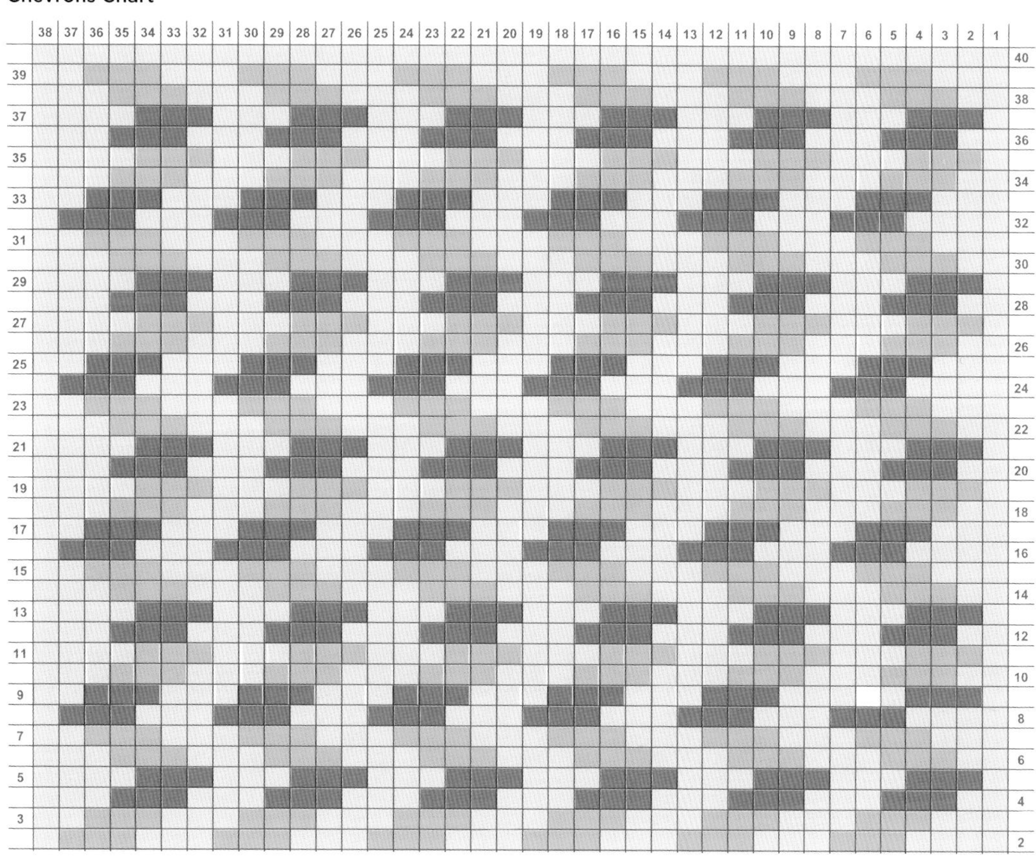

Crusader Chart

Highlander Chart

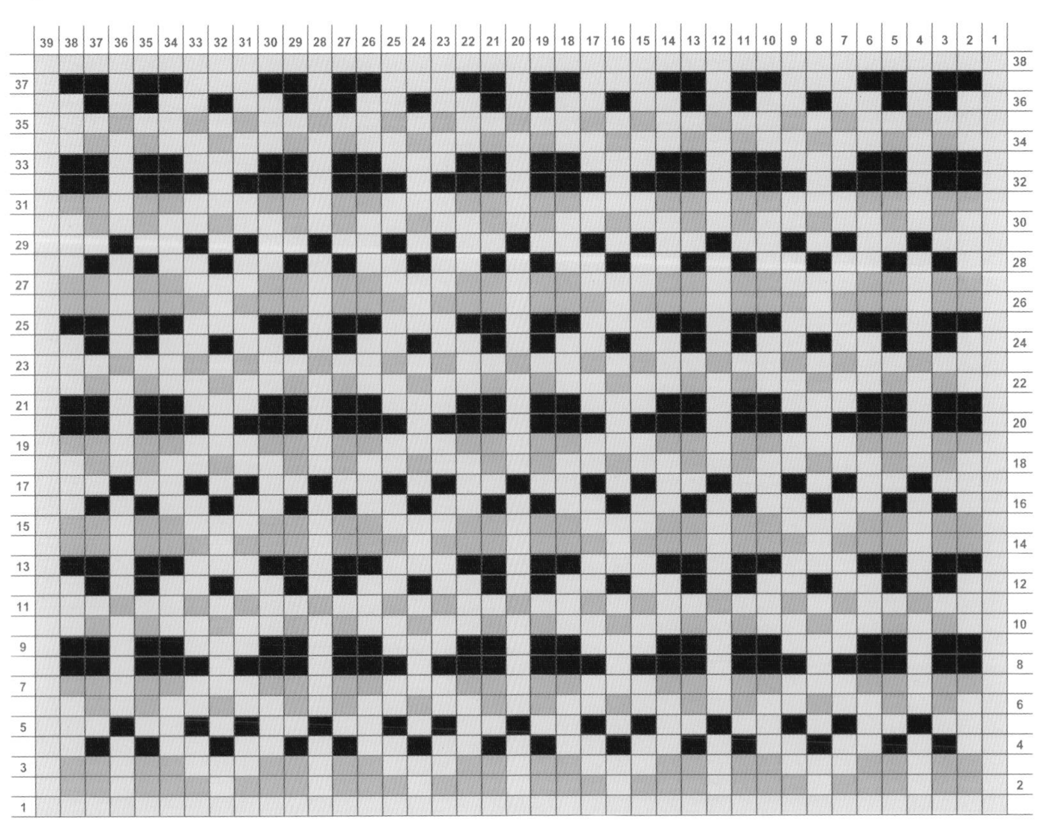

FIRTH WAVES CUSHION

by Jessie McKitrick

FINISHED MEASUREMENTS

19x19.75", to fit over 20" square pillow form.

YARN

Knit Picks Wool of the Andes Worsted Yarn (100% Peruvian Highland Wool; 110 yards/50g): C1 White 24065, 3 balls; C2 Spruce 23421, 2 balls; C3 Conch 25973, 1 ball; C4 Clarity 25632, 3 balls; C5 Icicle Heather 25992, 1 ball; C6 Marina 25074, 1 ball.

NEEDLES

US 7 (4.5mm) 24" circular needles, or size to obtain gauge

NOTIONS

Yarn Needle
Stitch Markers
20" Square Pillow Form

GAUGE

21 sts and 24 rounds = 4" in stranded St st in the round, blocked.

Firth Waves Cushion

Notes:

The word "firth" is Scots for an inlet or bay, and having enjoyed the beautiful Firth of Forth on a trip to Edinburgh, that seemed like the right choice for this cozy, wavy cushion.

The cushion is knit in the round, forming a tube that is then seamed closed at bottom and top edges over a pillow form. It has some negative ease in order to help the cushion retain its shape over time, as pillow forms tend to compress slightly with use.

For an extra pop of color, the pattern features one row per repeat of three colors in the same round. Carrying the third color may have an impact on your gauge, but as it is spaced regularly and evenly, taking care to spread out the right needle stitches evenly as you work can minimize this impact. For longer runs, twist the floating yarn with the working yarn every 5th st. Alternately, the third color stitches can also be embroidered afterward using duplicate stitching, though this method will result in many ends to weave-in later. If you are choosing to do this, simply omit color C3 while knitting and knit that stitch with color C6 instead as a placeholder.

When working the charts, each round is read from right to left. Work repeats of Chart A and B 33 times across the round, knitting all sts.

Duplicate Stitching

Using a length of yarn and a yarn needle, starting at the back of work, start your stitch at the base of the stitch you are covering (at the point of the 'V'). Bringing your working yarn through to the right side of work, work your stitch by threading the needle across through the back of the stitch above the one that you are covering. Finish the stitch by working through the base to the back of the work.

DIRECTIONS

With C1, CO 198 sts.
Being careful not to twist sts, join to work in the round, PM for beginning of round and work 1 round in C1.

Work from Chart A through row 8, then work from Chart B through row 14. Repeat these 22 rounds 4 more times, or until approximately 18.5" in length from CO edge.

Work one more repeat of Chart A.

BO loosely, using C1.

If you chose to omit color C3 in favor of duplicate stitching, duplicate stitch with lengths of color C3 according to placement on chart.

Finishing

Weave in ends, wash and block to measurements, with beginning and end of round lining up at the side of the cushion, to reduce visual impact of the jog that occurs here.

Using C1, employ Mattress Stitch to stitch lower edge closed, then weave in ends.

Insert pillow form, gently stretching cover into place.

Using C1, employ Mattress Stitch to stitch upper edge closed, then use duplicate stitch technique on a C1 area to secure yarn ends before tucking remaining ends into the inside of the cushion.

Chart A

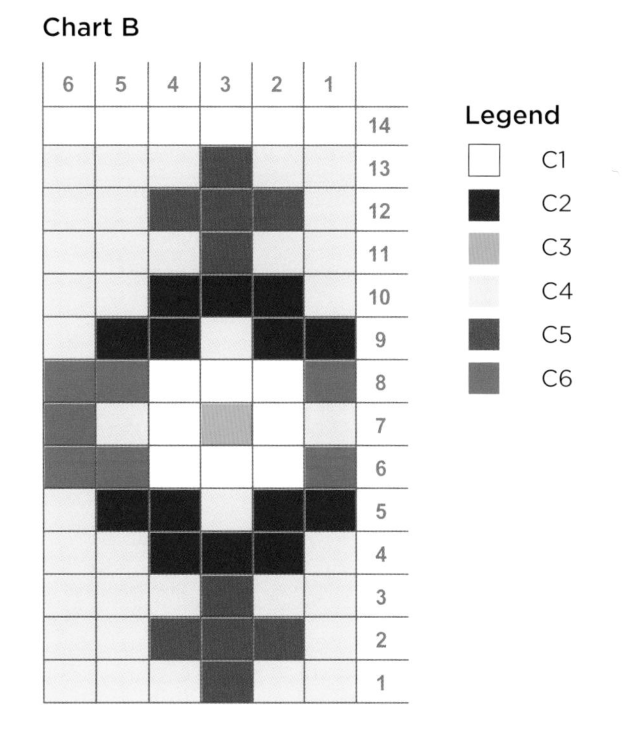

SILVERLING PILLOW

by Nataliya Galifianakis

FINISHED MEASUREMENTS

Approximately 15" square.

YARN

Knit Picks Wool of the Andes Sport (100% Peruvian Highland Wool, 137 yards/50g): C1 Dove Heather 25656, 3 balls; C2 Marina 25290, 1 ball; Midnight Heather 25661, 1 ball

NEEDLES

US 3 (3.25 mm) 16" or 24" circular needles, or size to obtain gauge

Extra knitting needle for three-needle bind off of same or one size smaller.

NOTIONS

Stitch Markers (2)

15" square pillow form

Five buttons approximately 1" in diameter

GAUGE

24 sts and 24 rows = 4" in Fair Isle pattern, blocked

Silverling Pillow

Notes:

The pillow is worked in one piece in the round starting at the lower edge. The stitches for the pillow are cast on provisionally. Front panel of the pillow is worked in Fair Isle Pattern. Back panel of the pillow is worked in the Stripe Pattern that uses the same two colors as the row in the front. Button band is worked as an extension of the front panel. Then, the stitches of the provisional cast-on are joined together with a three-needle bind off method. Five buttons fasten the button band on the back of the pillow. When working the charts, knit all sts and read each round from right to left, working pattern repeats as indicated.

Fair Isle Pattern (worked in the round over 91 sts in multiples of 13 sts)

Round 1: *K2A, K2B, K2A, K1B, K2A, K2B, K2A, repeat from * 7 times.

Rounds 2, 12: * K1A, K1C, K2A, K1C, K3A, K1C, K2A, K1C, K1A, repeat from * 7 times.

Rounds 3, 11: * K1A, K1C, K3A, K1C, K1A, K1C, K3A, K1C, K1A, repeat from * 7 times.

Rounds 4, 10: *K2A, K1C, K3A, K1C, K3A, K1C, K2A, repeat from 7 times.

Rounds 5, 9: *K3A, K1B, K2A, K1B, K2A, K1B, K3A, repeat from * 7 times.

Rounds 6, 8: *K1B, K4A, K3B, K4A, K1B, repeat from * 7 times.

Round 7: *K2B, K2A, K2B, K1A, K2B, K2A, K2B, repeat from * 7 times.

Repeat Rounds 1-12 for pattern.

Stripes Pattern (worked in the round over 90 sts in multiples of 4 plus 2 sts)

Rounds 1, 5, 7, 9: *K2B, K2A, repeat from * to the last two sts, K2B.

Rounds 2, 4, 10, 12: *K2A, K2C, repeat from * to the last two sts, K2A.

Rounds 3, 11: *K2C, K2A, repeat from * to the last two sts, K2C.

Rounds 6, 8: *K2A, K2B, repeat from * to the last two sts, K2A.

Repeat Rounds 1-12 for pattern.

Stripes Pattern (worked flat over multiples of 4 plus 2 sts)

Row 1, 7 (RS): *K2B, K2A, repeat from * to the last two sts, K2B.

Row 2, 8 (WS): *P2A, P2B, repeat from * to the last two sts, P2A.

Row 3, 5: *K2C, K2A, repeat from * to the last two sts, K2C.

Row 4, 6: *P2A, P2C, repeat from * to the last two sts, P2A.

Repeat Rows 1-8 for pattern.

3-Needle Bind Off

* Hold the two pieces of knitting together with the points facing to the right. Insert a third needle into the first stitch on each of the needles knitwise, starting with the front needle. Work a knit st, pulling the loop through both of the sts you've inserted the third needle through. After pulling the loop through, slip the first st off of each of the needles. Repeat from *. Pass the first finished st over the second and off of the needle.

DIRECTIONS

With yarn (A) provisionally cast on 181 sts. Knit 91 sts, place a marker, knit to the end of the row. Join to knit in the round and place a marker for the beginning of the round, being careful not to twist sts.

Pillow Body

Work Fair Isle Pattern Round 1 from the beginning of the round to the next marker, slip the marker, work Stripes Pattern (worked in the round) Round 1 to the end of the round. Continue as established until piece measures approximately 15" from the cast on edge finishing with Row 12 of the Stripes Pattern. Next, turn your work. With wrong side facing knit 90 sts with yarn (A), remove the marker between patterns, turn. With yarn (A) bind off 90 sts, remove the beginning of the round marker, K2tog, (90 sts remain on the needles).

Buttonhole Band

Beginning with a RS row, work in Stripes Pattern (worked flat, written directions only) for 8 rows. On the next two rows make buttonholes:

Row 1 (RS): With yarn (A) *K11, BO 5 sts, repeat from * to the last 10 sts, K10.

Row 2 (WS): With yarn (A) P10, CO 5 sts, *P11, CO 5 sts, repeat from * to the last 11 sts, P11.

Next, work rows 5-8 of Stripes Pattern (worked flat). Bind off all stitches.

Finishing

Unzip the provisionally cast on sts and divide them between two needles (91 sts on one needle and 90 sts on the other needle). Position the needles with stitches in parallel next to each other with wrong sides facing each other. Using third needle, bind off all the stitches with three-needle bind off method using yarn (A). Knit last st on left needle and BO. Pull yarn through final st to fasten off.

Weave in ends, wash and block to diagram.

Sew the buttons opposite buttonholes.

Stripes Pattern

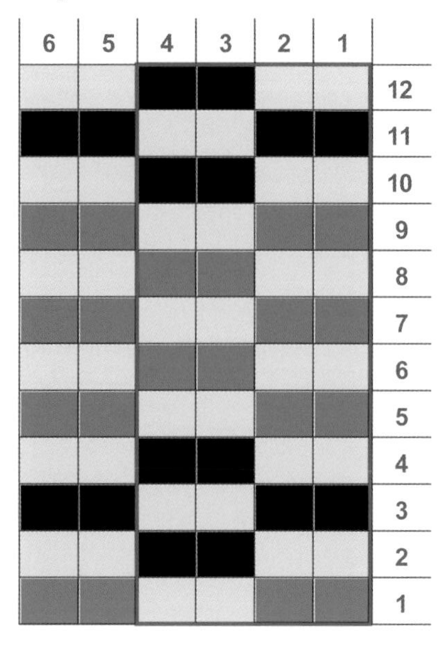

Fair Isle Pattern

Row	13	12	11	10	9	8	7	6	5	4	3	2	1
12	C1	C3	C1	C1	C3	C1	C1	C1	C3	C1	C1	C3	C1
11	C1	C3	C1	C1	C1	C3	C1	C3	C1	C1	C1	C3	C1
10	C1	C1	C3	C1	C1	C1	C3	C1	C1	C1	C3	C1	C1
9	C1	C1	C1	C2	C1	C1	C2	C1	C1	C2	C1	C1	C1
8	C2	C1	C1	C1	C1	C2	C2	C2	C1	C1	C1	C1	C2
7	C2	C2	C1	C1	C2	C2	C1	C2	C2	C1	C1	C2	C2
6	C2	C1	C1	C1	C1	C2	C2	C2	C1	C1	C1	C1	C2
5	C1	C1	C1	C2	C1	C1	C2	C1	C1	C2	C1	C1	C1
4	C1	C1	C3	C1	C1	C1	C3	C1	C1	C1	C3	C1	C1
3	C1	C3	C1	C1	C1	C3	C1	C3	C1	C1	C1	C3	C1
2	C1	C3	C1	C1	C3	C1	C1	C1	C3	C1	C1	C3	C1
1	C1	C1	C2	C2	C1	C1	C2	C1	C1	C2	C2	C1	C1

Legend

- C1
- C2
- C3
- Pattern Repeat

GLACIER BAY PILLOW COVER

by Robin Nickerson

FINISHED MEASUREMENTS

Approximately 23" around and 14" high (to fit 12"x 12" pillow form)

YARN

Knit Picks Palette (100% Peruvian Highland Wool; 231 yards/50g): (MC) Cream 23730, 2 balls; (C1) Seafaring 26048, (C2) Spruce 25535, and (C3) Caribbean 25095, 1 ball each.

NEEDLES

US 2 (3mm) 24" circular needle, or size to obtain gauge

NOTIONS

Blocking Pins
Yarn Needle
Stitch Marker
12"x 12" pillow form

GAUGE

28 sts and 32 rows = 4" in stranded Stockinette Stitch in the round, blocked. For this project do not go bigger than a size US 3 (3.25mm) needle (the pillow cover needs a dense fabric).
Adding (or subtracting) CO stitches in increments of 8 is the preferred way to adjust the size.

Glacier Bay Pillow Cover

Notes:

The pillow cover is worked in stranded stockinette stitch in the round forming a tube. When the height of the tube is sufficient to cover the pillow insert, the cover is bound off. The bottom edge is seamed first, the pillow form is inserted, and then the top edge is seamed.

For this design the MC Cream yarn is the background color, and the colored yarns are considered the dominant colors. This means the colored yarns should be stranded under the cream yarn in order to obtain the sharpest contrast.

When the chart indicates a color change, break the old color leaving a 3" tail. At the end of the project the yarn tails will be tied together and left inside the pillow cover.

DIRECTIONS

CO 160 sts with MC Cream. Join in the round and place a stitch marker to indicate the beginning of the round, being careful not to twist sts.

Bottom Edge (using MC)

Rounds 1, 3: Knit.
Rounds 2, 4: Purl.

Main Body

Begin working the Glacier Bay Chart in the round, knitting each stitch and reading the Chart from right to left. The white blocks designate the background color, and the shaded blocks designate the colored yarn.

Work Glacier Bay Chart Round 1, repeating the 16 sts 10 times across the round; slip the stitch marker, and begin Round 2

Begin the chart by using C3 Caribbean as the contrasting color (MC Cream is the background color throughout). Continue with C3 Caribbean until the chart changes from black shaded blocks to gray shaded blocks. This change in shading indicates the round where the next contrasting color (C1 Seafaring) should begin. Continue with C1 Seafaring until the next color change is indicated (by a switch from gray to black shaded blocks), and change to C2 Spruce. When the C2 Spruce section is completed, the color sequence will begin again with C3 Caribbean.

The chart has a 42 round repeat so when the 42nd round is finished, change to the next Contrasting Color in the sequence and begin with round 1 again.

Continue working through as many color sequences as necessary to approximately equal the height of the pillow insert without stretching. Finish with one of the rounds before a color change, either 10, 21, 31, or 42.

Break off the final contrasting color yarn, and continue the top edging with MC Cream (to match the bottom edge).

Top Edge (using MC)

Round 1, 3: K.
Round 2, 4: P.
Round 5: BO, leaving a 32" tail for seaming.

Finishing

On the WS of the cover, tie together the ends of the colored yarns where the color changes occurred. Do not cut the ends short, leave them inside the tube where they will rub against each other, slightly felting, thus becoming perfectly secure.

Wet block the pillow cover so that the dimensions are about 12" in width and about 14" in height (when laid flat). This will allow length for seaming and for the cover to fit the rounded contours of the pillow form.

When your pillow cover is completely dry, thread the yarn needle with a length of MC Cream yarn (or use the CO tail if it is long enough), and with wrong sides together, seam the bottom edges of the pillow cover together. Weave the end of the seaming thread to the inside of the pillow cover.

Place the pillow form inside the cover so that the long edge of the pillow form matches up with the long edge of the bottom seam. Adjust the cover so that the top edges meet over the top of the pillow in the same manner as the bottom edges.
Use the yarn needle threaded with the BO tail to seam the top edges together.

The top edges will be trickier to seam because they are under tension. Seaming might be easier if you baste or pin the edges first.

Sew the final seam, securing it with a couple of knots at the end, and hide the tail of the seaming thread by poking it to the inside of the pillow cover.

Glacier Bay Chart

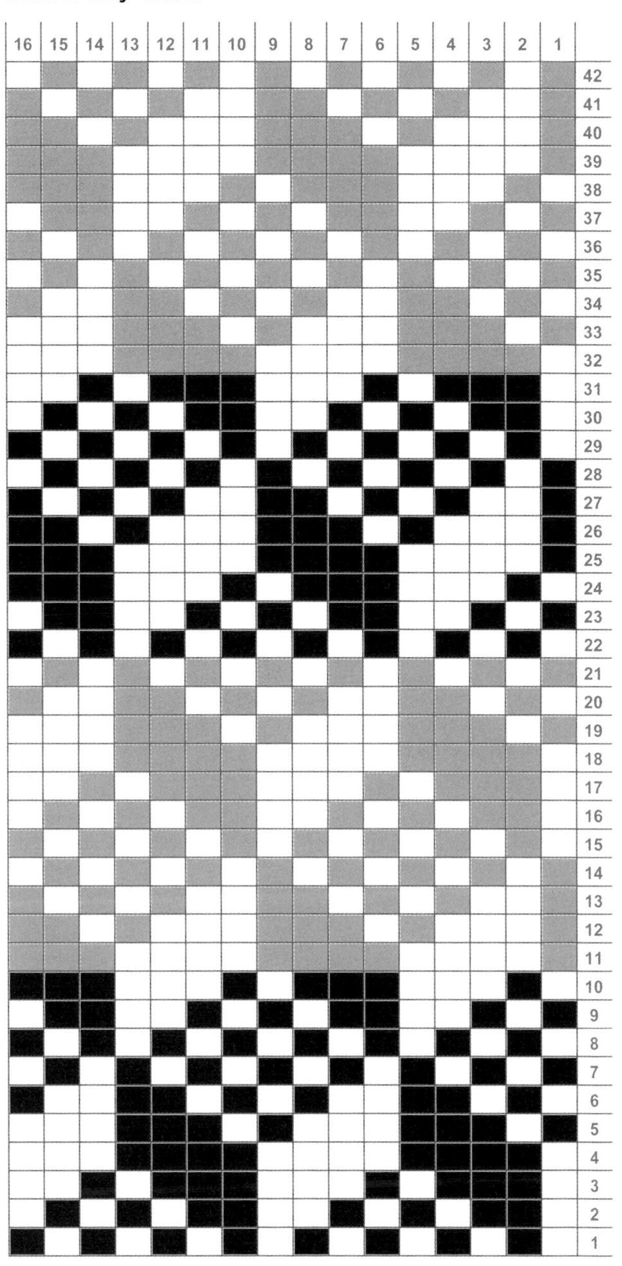

Work the Glacier Bay Chart in the round, knitting each stitch and reading the Chart from right to left.

Work Glacier Bay Chart Round 1, repeating the 16 sts 10 times across the round; slip the stitch marker, and begin Round 2.

Begin by using C3 Caribbean as the contrasting color (MC Cream is the background color throughout). Continue with C3 Caribbean until the chart changes from black shaded blocks to gray shaded blocks. This change in shading indicates the round where the next contrasting color (C1 Seafaring) should begin. Continue with C1 Seafaring until the next color change is indicated (by a switch from gray to black shaded blocks), and change to C2 Spruce. When the C2 Spruce section is completed, the color sequence will begin again with C3 Caribbean.

The chart has a 42 round repeat so when the 42nd round is finished, change to the next Contrasting Color in the sequence and begin with round 1 again.

Continue working through as many color sequences as necessary to approximately equal the height of the pillow insert without stretching. Finish with one of the rounds before a color change, either 10, 21, 31, or 42.

Break off the final contrasting color yarn, and continue the top edging with MC Cream (to match the bottom edge).

TUDOR WINTER MITTS & TOQUE

by Rhonda Black

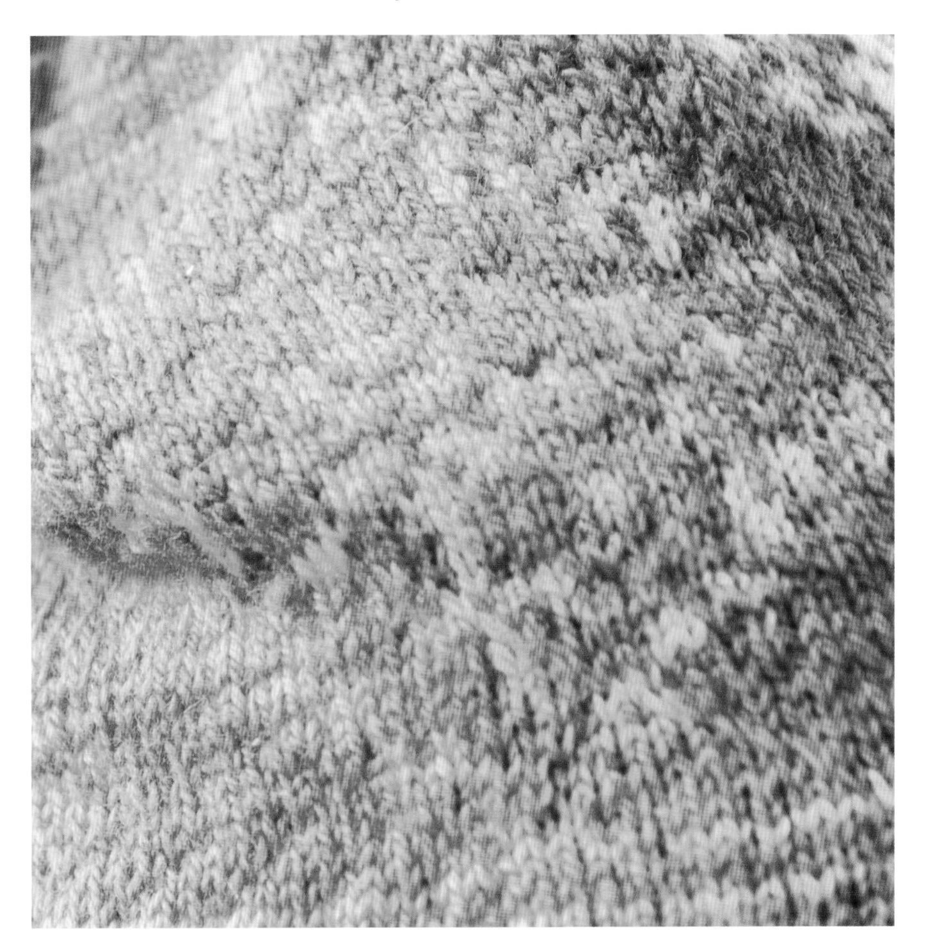

FINISHED MEASUREMENTS

Sizes: S (M/L) Toque: 19 (20)" brim, 21" head circumference; 11.5" length (including brim)
Sizes S (M) Mitts: 6.5 (7)" wrist, 9.5" length (including cuff), 7.5" palm circumference

YARN

Knit Picks Palette (100% Peruvian Highland Wool; 231 yards/50g): MC Rouge 24567, 3 balls; C1 Canary 25531, 3 balls

NEEDLES

US 2 (2.75mm) DPNs or long circular needle for Magic Loop technique, or size to obtain gauge

NOTIONS

Yarn Needle
Stitch Markers (one different color)
Waste Yarn

GAUGE

32 sts and 36 rows = 4" in stranded Corrugated Rib and stranded St st in the round, blocked.

Tudor Winter Toque & Mitts

Notes:
Toque and Mitts are knit in the round using stranded stockinette; sizing of Mitts correlates to wrist circumference only. The ribbing for the Toque begins with K1 in MC, while the Mitts ribbing begins with P in C1. For longer color repeats, catch unused color strands every 3-4 sts. When knitting a single color round, carry unused color up at join. While optional, use the Jogless Join technique for more finished appearance between rounds. The charts are marked for Jogless Join. Always read charts from right to left when working in the round, knitting all sts.

Corrugated Rib for Toque (in the round over an even number of sts)
Round 1: *K1 with MC, bring C1 to front, P1 with C1, take C1 to back; rep from * to end of round.
Repeat Round 1 for pattern.

Corrugated Rib for Mitts (in the round over an even number of sts)
Round 1: *With C1 in front, P1 with C1, take C1 to back. K1 with MC; rep from * to end of round.
Repeat Round 1 for pattern.

Jogless Join Technique
Note: Slip all sts purlwise. Marker 'A' (MA) is different color than other markers used and will move one st to left at end of every round.
Preparation
Step 1: Mark charted patt: Place mark between first and second sts on chart. Cont marking spaces between each st, up one round and one st to left like stairsteps, to indicate where MA will be placed after each round.
Step 2: CO sts indicated by patt and join, being careful not to twist sts.
Round 1: After completing Corrugated Ribbing in instructions, SL first st after join. Place MA and knit to end of round, following marked patt.
Next Rounds: Remove MA, SL next st, replace MA, and knit to end of new marked round. Cont around in this manner through end of chart.
Since rounds are no longer knit in 'spirals', the floating sts at beg and end of rounds to right and left are eliminated.

Kitchener Stitch (grafting)
1: Pull yarn needle kwise through front stitch and drop stitch from knitting needle.
2: Pull yarn needle pwise through next front stitch, leave stitch on knitting needle.
3: Pull yarn needle pwise through first back stitch and drop stitch from knitting needle.
4: Pull yarn needle kwise through next back stitch, leave stitch on knitting needle.
Repeat steps 1 – 4 until all stitches have been grafted.

DIRECTIONS

TOQUE

With MC, loosely CO 152 (160) sts. Place MA to indicate beg of round and join, taking care not to twist sts.

Brim

Round 1: *K1, P1; rep from * to end of round.
Next Rounds: Join C1 and work Corrugated Rib for Toque until piece measures 2" from beg.
Next Round: With MC, *K1, P1; rep from * to end of round. Change to St st.

Setup Rounds
Round 1 Size Small only: *K9, M1, K19, M1, K10; rep from * 4 times. 8 sts inc. (160 sts).
Round 1 Size Medium/Large only: Knit to end of round.
Round 2: Knit to end.
Round 3: *K10, M1, K20, M1, K10; rep from * 4 times. 8 sts inc. (168 sts)
Round 4-5: Knit to end.

Body and Crown

Remove marker, SL next st, place MA and follow Jogless Join throughout chart.
Complete Rounds 1-78 of Toque Chart, working each chart row 4 times across the round. 16 sts.
Next Round: Cut yarn, leaving 9" tail of MC. With blunt needle, thread tail through rem sts twice, pull tog tightly, and secure.

Finishing

Weave in ends and wet block to measurements.

MITTS

Left Mitt

With MC, loosely CO 52 (56) sts and divide over needles as desired. Place MA for beg of round and join, being careful not to twist sts.

Cuff
Round 1: With MC, *P1, K1; rep from * to end of round.
Next Rounds: Join C1 and work Corrugated Rib for Mitts until piece measures 2" from beg.

Setup Rounds
Round 1: With MC only, *P1, K1; rep from * to end of round.
Round 2 Size Small only: K6, *M1, K13, rep from * 3 times, M1, K7. 4 sts inc. 56 sts.
Round 2 Size Medium/Large only: Knit to end of round.
Round 3: Knit to end of round.
Round 4: K7, *M1, K14, rep from * 3 times, M1, K7. 4 sts inc. 60 sts.

Hand
Remove MA, SL next st, place MA and follow Jogless Join throughout. Work Chart 1 Hand Rounds 1-15.

Thumb Placement
Round 16: Work 16 sts in patt. Join waste yarn and K13 sts onto waste yarn. Sl waste yarn sts back to LH needle. Con't knitting

in Round 16 patt, including the waste yarn sts again, to end of round.

Next Rounds: Cont working Chart 1 Hand through Round 62. 20 sts.
Place first 10 sts on needle, and rem sts on separate needle (DPN or circular needles, as preferred). Cut yarns, leaving 7" tail of C1 for grafting. Position needles perpendicular to one another. With yarn needle, graft these sts tog using kitchener stitch.

Left Thumb

With needle #1, slide needle into first leg of each st directly below waste yarn. Next, slide needle #2 into first leg of 13 sts above waste yarn. Carefully remove waste yarn with yarn needle. 26 sts, 13 on each needle.
With extra DPN, pick up 1 st between needles #1 and #2 on the right hand side and place st on needle #1. Repeat on left hand side of thumb hole, placing st on needle #2. 28 sts.

Begin Thumb Charts 2 and 3

Beg with needle #1, rejoin C1.
Round 1: Work Chart 2 Thumb Palm Side Row 1, then Round 1 of Chart 3 Thumb Back Side to end of round. 26 sts.
Arrange 26 thumb sts onto needles as desired and place MA to indicate beg of round.
Next Rounds: Cont Rounds 2-23 similarly (i.e., Round 2 of Chart 2, Round 2 of Chart 3) through Round 23. 6 sts.

Cut yarn, leaving 6" tail of C1. Thread tail through yarn needle and graft rem sts tog using kitchener st. Use MC tail at base of thumb to close any gaps where thumb joins hand.

Right Mitt

Work Cuff and Set Up Rounds as for Left Mitt.

Hand

Work Chart 1 as for Left Mitt, through Round 15.

Thumb Placement

Round 16: K1 in C1, K1 in MC, join waste yarn, K13 sts onto waste yarn. SL waste yarn sts back to LH needle. Cont knitting in Round 16 of patt, including waste yarn sts again, to end of round.
Next Rounds: Cont Rounds 17-62. Finish as for Left Mitt.

Right Thumb

PU thumb sts, remove waste yarn, and place extra end sts on needles as for Left Mitt.

Begin Thumb Charts 3 and 2

With needle #1 and C1, work Round 1 of Chart 3 Thumb Back Side and Round 1 of Chart 2 Thumb Palm Side to end of round. Arrange 26 thumb sts onto needles as desired. Place MA to indicate beg of round. (26 sts)
Next Rounds: Cont in same manner for Rounds 2-23, through end of chart. (6 sts)

Cut yarns and finish as for Left thumb.

Finishing

Weave in ends and wet block to measurements.

Mitts - Chart 1

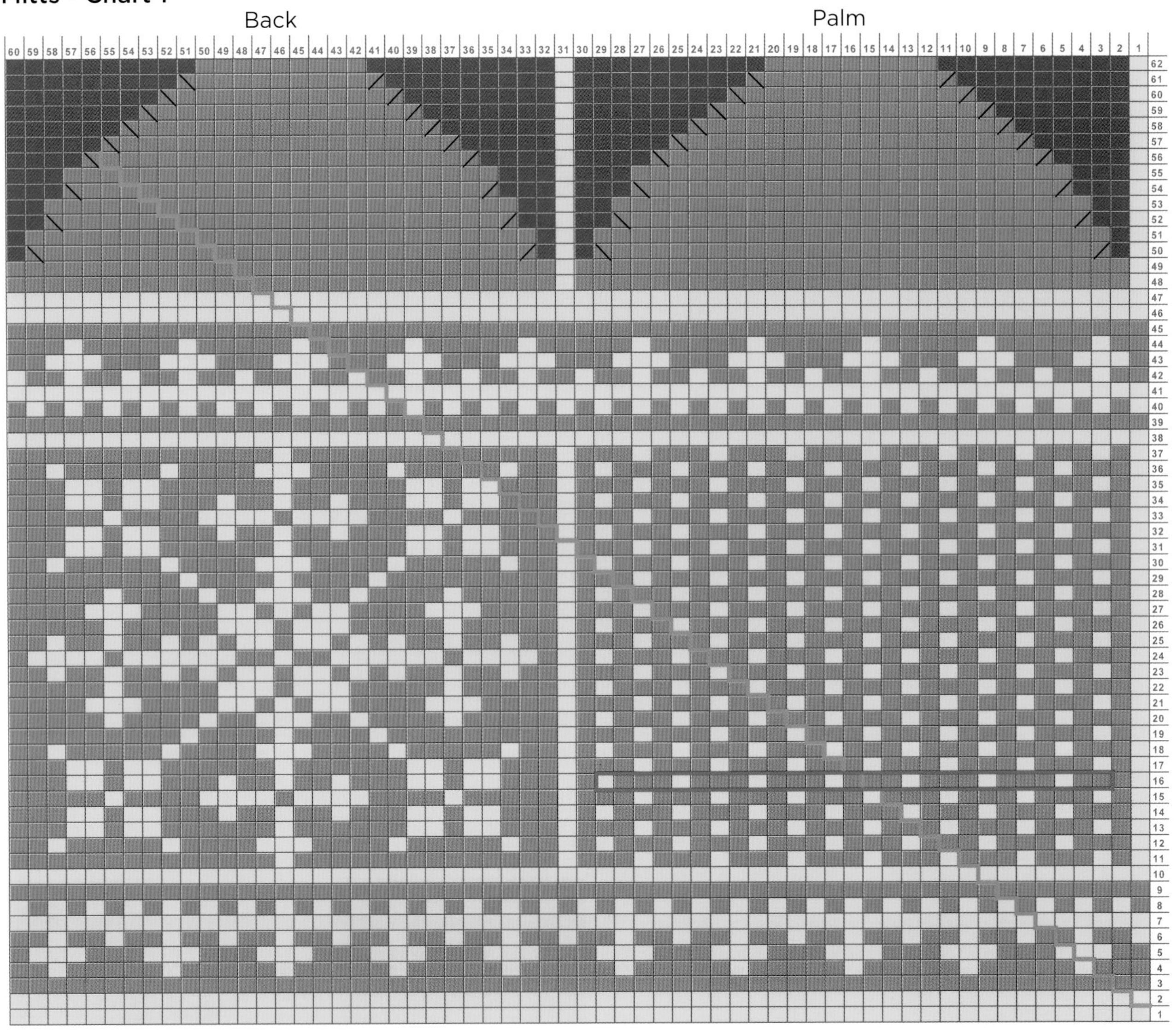

Thumb Palm - Chart 2

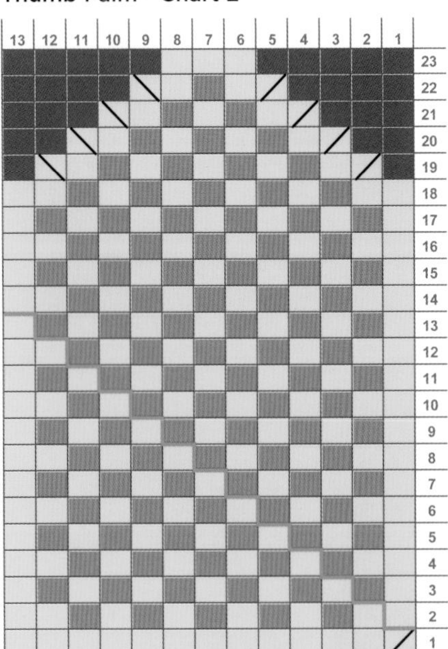

Thumb Back - Chart 3

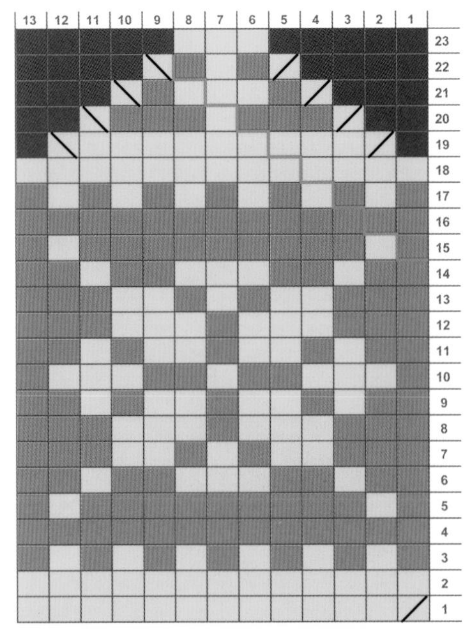

Toque Chart

Legend

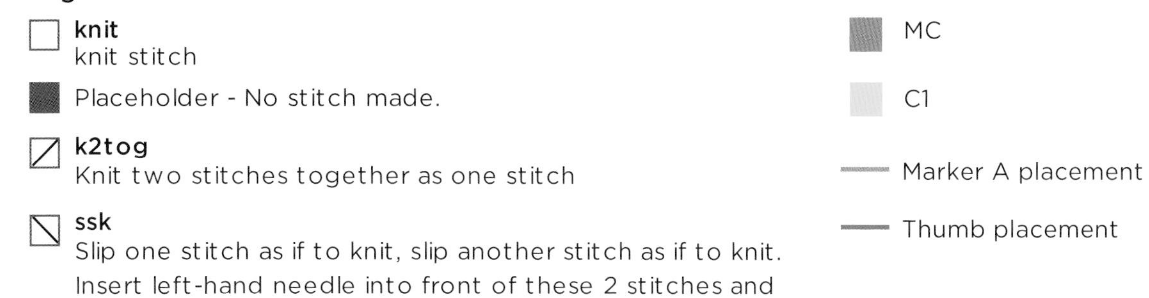

FAIR ISLE EARFLAP HAT & COWL

by Jenny Williams

FINISHED MEASUREMENTS
Hat: 19.5 (21.75, 24)" circumference
Cowl: 24" circumference x 6" tall

YARN
Knit Picks Wool of the Andes Worsted Yarn (100% Peruvian Highland Wool; 110 yards/50g), 1 skein each: C1 Garnet Heather 25633; C2 Brass Heather 25638; C3 Firecracker Heather 23896; C4 Spruce 23421; C5 Oyster Heather 24649; C6 Dove Heather 24077.

NEEDLES
US 6 (4mm) set of DPNs or two 24" circular needles for two circulars technique, or one 32" or longer circular needle for Magic Loop
US 4 (3.5mm) circular or straight needles, or two sizes smaller than gauge needle

NOTIONS
Yarn Needle
Stitch Markers, 1 of a different color

GAUGE
22 sts and 28 rows = 4" in stranded St st in the round, blocked, using larger needles.

Fair Isle Earflap Hat & Cowl

Notes:

With one set of yarn (6 skeins), you can make any 2 items; one using Chart A and the other using Chart B. Directions are given for both options. Both the Hat and the Cowl are worked in the round on circular needles. Earflaps are worked flat and will resemble bows, which are folded in half for double thickness. When working the charts, follow all rows from right to left for working in the round, knitting each st.

Knitted Cast On
Begin with a slip knot on the LN. Knit one st into the slip knot, sliding the newly knit stitch back onto the LN. Repeat for the number of sts required.

Seed St (worked in the round over an odd number of sts)
Round 1: *K1, P1; repeat from * to end, ending with K1.
Row 2 and every row thereafter: K the purls sts, and P the knit sts.

DIRECTIONS

HAT AND COWL USING CHART A

Hat sizes are shown as 1st, 2nd and 3rd numbers listed, the fourth number is for the Cowl. Using the knitted cast on method, with larger circular needles and C4, CO 108 (120, 132, 132) sts. PM to indicate the beginning of the round. Join, to begin working in the round, taking care to not twist sts.

Bottom Braid Edging, Chart A
Round 1: *K1 in C2, K1 in C4; repeat from * to end of round.
Round 2: Bring both yarns to front of work. *P1 in C2, cross strand of C4 over strand just worked, P1 in C4, cross C2 over C4; repeat from * to end of round.
Round 3: Starting with C4, work as for Round 2, but cross strand just worked UNDER strand to be worked.

Hat & Cowl Body, Chart A

Switch to C1 and knit 1 (1, 1, 2) round(s). Work the 40 rounds of Chart A. Mark the beginning of each pattern repeat with a stitch marker, using a different color marker than was used for the beginning of round stitch marker. Each chart row will be repeated 9 (10, 11, 11) times on each round. (For Cowl, skip to Cowl Finishing after completing chart.)

Crown Shaping, Chart A
Switch to DPNs or Magic Loop as needed.
Step 1: Continuing with C1, *K to 2 sts before marker, K2tog, SM; repeat from * 9 (10, 11) times total. 9 (10, 11) sts dec. 99 (111, 123) sts. Knit 3 rounds.

Step 2: *K to 2 sts before marker, K2tog, SM; repeat from * 9, (10, 11) times. Knit 2 rounds. Repeat Step 2 1 (1, 2) more time(s). 81 (91, 90) sts.

Step 3: *K to 2 sts before marker, K2tog, SM; repeat from * 9, (10, 11) times. Knit 1 round. Repeat Step 3 1 (2, 2) more time(s). 63 (61, 57) sts.

Step 4: K2tog across round, removing st markers as you go. An uneven number of sts may be left at the end of the round, if that is the case end with K1. 32 (31, 29) sts.

Repeat Step 4 two more times. 8 sts left.

Cut 4" tail and thread through remaining sts, pulling tight to close hole. Weave in tail.

Earflap, Chart A (Make 2)

Using smaller needles and C4, CO 25 sts.

Decrease Rows:
Row 1: K3, work Seed st for 19 sts, K3.
Row 2: P3, Seed st 19, P3.
Row 3: K1, K2tog tbl, Seed st to last 3 sts, K2tog, K1. 2 sts dec.
Row 4: P2, Seed st to last 2 sts, P2.
Repeat Rows 3 and 4 until 5 sts remain. P5.

Increase Rows:
Row 1: K2, M1, work Seed st to last 2 sts, M1, K2. 2 sts inc.
Row 2: P2, Seed st to last 2 sts, P2.
Row 3: Repeat Row 1.
Row 4: P3, Seed st to last 3 sts, P3.
Repeat Rows 1 - 4 5 times. 25 sts total. Bind off all sts.

Fold Earflap in half, wrong sides together, forming a triangle. Using C4 threaded into a yarn needle, embroider in blanket stitch around the open edges.

Hat Finishing

Weave in ends. Block Hat Body and allow to dry thoroughly. Pin Earflaps over your ears and sew in place, just under braided edge.

Cowl Finishing, Chart A

Knit 3 rounds in C1, removing st markers as you go.
Top Braid Edging (for Cowl only)
Repeat Bottom Braid Edging, Chart A.
Bind off all sts using C4.
Weave in ends. Block Cowl around rolled up towels and allow to dry thoroughly.

HAT AND COWL USING CHART B

Hat sizes are shown as 1st, 2nd and 3rd numbers listed, the fourth number is for the Cowl. Using the knitted cast on method, with larger circular needles and C3, CO 108 (120, 132, 132) sts. PM to indicate the beginning of the round. Join, to begin working in the round, taking care to not twist sts.

Bottom Braid Edging, Chart B
Round 1: *K1 in C5, K1 in C3; repeat from * to end of round.

Round 2: Bring both yarns to front of work. *P1 in C5, cross strand of C3 over strand just worked, P1 in C3, cross C5 over C3. Repeat from * to end of round.

Round 3: Starting with C3, work as for Round 2, but cross strand just worked UNDER strand to be worked.

Hat & Cowl Body, Chart B

Continuing with C5, knit 1 (1, 1, 2) round(s). Work the 40 rounds of Chart B. Mark the beginning of each pattern repeat with a stitch marker, using a different color marker than was used for the beginning of round stitch marker. Each chart row will be repeated 9 (10, 11, 11) times on each round.

For Cowl, skip to Cowl Finishing after completing chart.

Crown Shaping

Continuing with C5, work Crown Shaping as for Hat and Cowl Chart A.

Earflap, Chart B (Make 2)

Using smaller needles and C5, CO 25 sts.
Make Earflap as for Hat and Cowl Chart A. Use C5 to embroider the blanket stitch.

Hat Finishing

Weave in ends. Block Hat Body and allow to dry thoroughly. Pin Earflaps over your ears and sew in place, just under braided edge.

Cowl Finishing for Chart B

Knit 3 rounds in C5, removing st markers as you go.

Top Braid Edging (for Cowl only)

Repeat Bottom Braid Edging, Chart B. Bind off all sts using C3. Weave in ends. Block Cowl around rolled up towels and allow to dry thoroughly.

Chart A

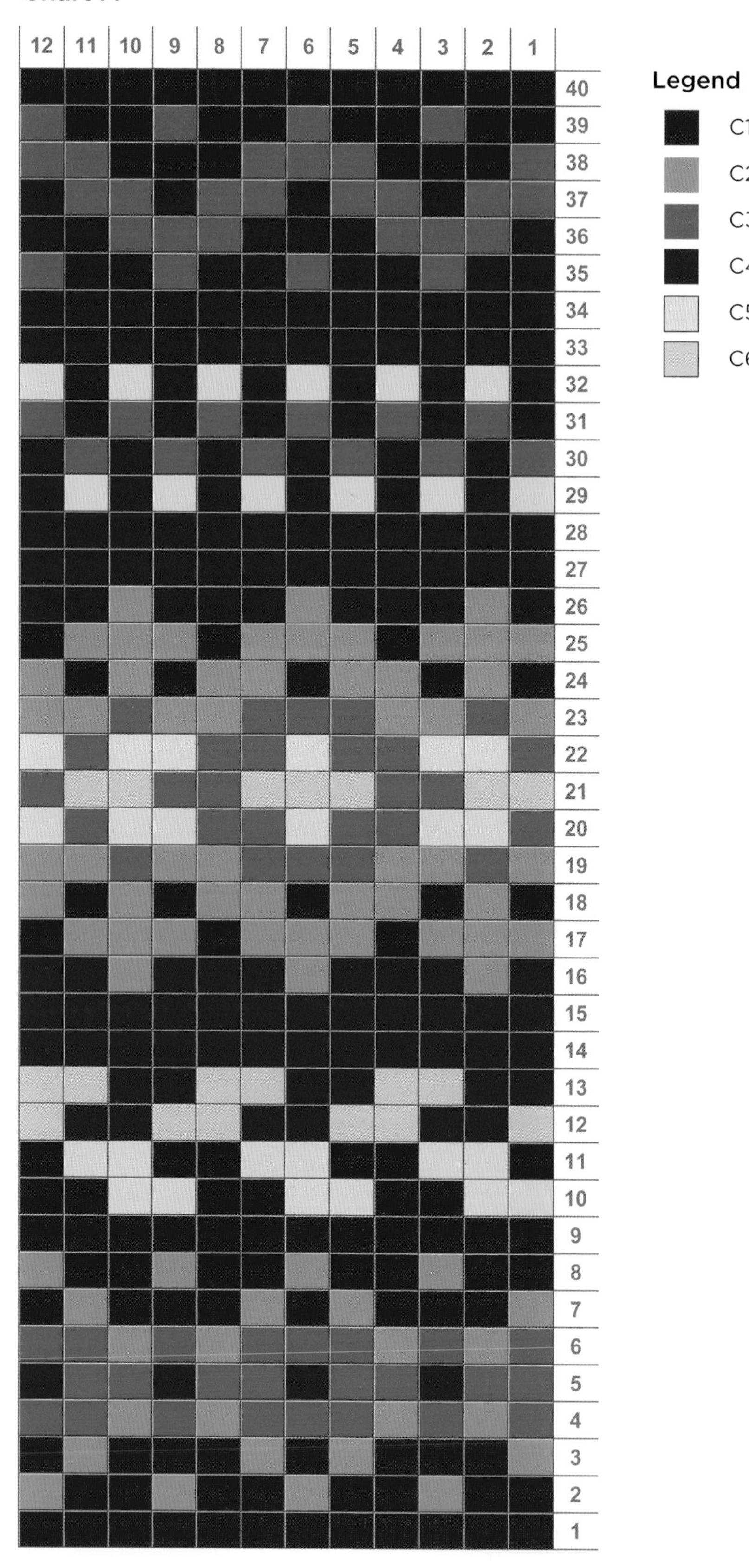

12 11 10 9 8 7 6 5 4 3 2 1
40 39 38 37 36 35 34 33 32 31 30 29 28 27 26 25 24 23 22 21 20 19 18 17 16 15 14 13 12 11 10 9 8 7 6 5 4 3 2 1
Legend
C1
C2
C3
C4
C5
C6

Chart B

12 11 10 9 8 7 6 5 4 3 2 1

40 39 38 37 36 35 34 33 32 31 30 29 28 27 26 25 24 23 22 21 20 19 18 17 16 15 14 13 12 11 10 9 8 7 6 5 4 3 2 1

MUSKOKA HAT AND MITTS

by Brenda Castiel

FINISHED MEASUREMENTS

Hat Circumference: 17.5 (19.5)"; Height: 14" plus pompom
Mittens Circumference: 6.5 (7.5)"
Pattern is written for Small/Medium to fit a youth, and a Medium/Large to fit an average sized adult.

YARN

Knit Picks Wool of the Andes Worsted (100% Wool; 110 yards /50g):
MC Clarity 25632, 2 skeins; C1 Marina 25074, C2 Conch 25973, C3 Turmeric 25651, C4 Hollyberry 23419; 1 skein each.

NEEDLES

US 6 (4.0 mm) 16" circular needle, plus DPNs of same size, or two 24" circular needles for two circulars technique, or one 32" or longer circular needle for Magic Loop technique, or size to obtain gauge.

NOTIONS

Yarn Needle
Stitch Markers
Scrap Yarn or Stitch Holder

GAUGE

22 sts and 26 rows = 4" in stranded Stockinette stitch in the round, blocked.

Muskoka Hat and Mittens

Notes:

In Canada a longish knit winter hat, or stocking cap, is called a toque, or sometimes tuque (pronounced "tuke").

This version is covered with non-traditional fair-isle designs, such as checkerboards, diamonds and chevrons, and is topped with a jaunty pompom. It comes with matching mittens.

The changing patterns and colors will give the knitter enough of a challenge to keep moving along.

Be sure to keep your floats loose, or the hat will be too tight. Where the float is 5 sts long, twist the 2 yarns together after the 2nd or 3rd st to keep the floats neat.

When working the charts, each round is read from right to left.

DIRECTIONS

Hat

Note: Change to DPNs when sts no longer fit on 16" circular needle.

With MC, loosely CO 92 (104) stitches. Join to work in the round, being careful not to twist sts. PM to indicate beg of round.

Round 1: *K1, p1, rep from * around.
Round 2: *K1 tbl, p1, rep from * around.
Rounds 3-20: Rep Rounds 1-2 nine more times.
Round 21: *K21, kfb, rep from * 4 times, k4 (16). 96 (108) sts.
Round 22: With C4, knit.
Round 23: Purl.
Round 24: Knit.
Rounds 25-50: Work Rounds 1-26 of Chart A, rep chart 16 (18) times across the round.
Round 51: Work Round 27 of Chart A as follows: *k6 (7) sts in pat, k2tog, rep from * around. 84 (96) sts.
Rounds 52-57: Work Rounds 28-33 of Chart A.
Round 58: Work Round 34 of Chart A as follows: *K5 (6) sts in pat, k2tog, rep from * around. 72 (84) sts.
Rounds 59-60: Work Rounds 35-36 of Chart A.
Round 61: Work Round 37 of Chart A as follows: *K16 (8) sts in pat, k2tog, rep from * to last 0 (4) sts, k0 (4). 68 (76) sts.
Rounds 62-67: Work Rounds 38-43 of Chart A, ending with stitch 2 (4) of the chart.
Round 68: Work Round 44 of Chart A as follows: *P5, p2tog, rep from * to last 12 (6) sts, p12 (6). 60 (66) sts.
Rounds 69-73: Work Rounds 45-49 of Chart A.
Round 74: Work Round 50 of Chart A as follows: *K4, k2tog, rep from * to last 0 (6) sts, k0 (6). 50 (56) sts.
Rounds 75-76: Work Rounds 51-52 of Chart A, ending with stitch 2 of the chart.
Round 77: Work Round 53 of Chart A as follows: *K4(5), k2tog, rep from * to last 2 (0) sts, k2 (0). 42 (48) sts.
Rounds 78-81: Work Rounds 54-57 of Chart A.

Shape Top

Round 82: With MC, knit.
Round 83: With C2, *k4, k2tog, rep from *. 35 (40) sts.
Round 84: Purl.
Round 85: Knit.
Round 86: With C1, *k3, k2tog, rep from *. 28 (32) sts.
Rounds 87-88: Knit.
Round 89: *K4, k2tog, rep from *, k4 (2). 24 (27) sts.
Round 90: *K3, k2tog, rep from *, k4 (2). 20 (22) sts.
Round 91: *K2, k2tog, rep from *, k0 (2). 15 (17) sts.
Round 92: K1, k2tog to end. 8 (9) sts.
Cut yarn, leaving 6 to 8 inch tail. Using yarn needle, draw yarn through rem sts. Pull tight and stitch down on WS.

Finishing

Weave in all loose yarn ends. Tack down any loose floats. Block hat.

Pompom

To make pompom, take a 3 inch wide piece of cardboard. Lay a length of yarn (in MC) along the length of the cardboard (this yarn will be used hold the pompom together and attach it to the hat). Wind yarn around the cardboard about 100 - 120 times, using one color or mixed colors. Pull the original length of yarn towards the lower edge of the cardboard, pull firmly around the wound yarn, and tie up tightly. With scissors, cut along the upper edge of the cardboard to free up the yarn. Trim ends to create a nice round shape. Use the tied ends to sew the pompom to the top of the hat

Mittens

Note: This pattern makes long mittens that continue past the wrist. For shorter mittens, omit one color section, e.g. rows 1 through 7 of the chart.

With MC, loosely CO 36 (42) stitches. Join to work in the round, being careful not to twist sts. PM to indicate beg of round.
Round 1: *K1, p1, rep from * around.
Round 2: *K1 tbl, p1, rep from * around.
Rounds 3- 12: Rep Rounds 1-2 five more times.
Round 13: Knit.
Round 14: With C4, knit.
Round 15: Purl.
Round 16: Knit.
Rounds 17-33: Work Rounds 1-17 of Chart A.
Round 34: Work round 18 of Chart A as follows: K2, kfb 0 (1) time, k32 (36) sts in pat, kfb 0 (1) time, k to end of round. 36 (44) sts.
Round 35 (begin thumb gusset): Work Round 19 of Chart A to last st, kfb (newly made st is Round 1 of Gusset Chart, PM before this st to mark Gusset). 37 (45) sts.
Note: Use colors on Chart A to stripe gusset unless directions instruct otherwise. Yarn not in use will form long floats - these floats should be caught with yarn being used every few sts. Any loose floats can be sewn down at the end.
Rounds 36-46 (48): Cont in patt, working Rounds 20-30 (32) of Chart A at beg of round and Rounds 2-12 (14) of Gusset Chart at end of round. 47 (57) sts.
Round 47 (49): Work Round 31 (33) of Chart A to beg of gusset, place 11 (13) gusset sts on holder or scrap yarn. 36 (44) sts.

Size S/M:
Rounds 48-49: Work Rounds 32-33 of Chart A.
Round 50: With MC, knit.

Round 51: Purl.

Rounds 52-60: Work Rounds 45-53 of Chart A.

Size M/L:

Round 50: With C2, work Round 34 of Chart A as: K2, k2tog, k36 sts in pat, k2tog, k to end of round in pat. 42 sts.

Rounds 51-69: Work Rounds 35-53 of Chart A.

Both Sizes continue with Round 70:

Round 70: With MC work Round 54 of Chart A as, *K1, k2tog, k13 (17) sts in pat, ssk, pm, rep from * once more to end of round. 32 (38) sts.

Round 71: Work Chart A Round 55 in pat.

Round 72: Work Chart A Round 56 as: *K1, k2tog, work in pat to 2 sts before marker, ssk, sm, rep from *. 28 (34) sts.

Round 73: Work Chart A Round 57 in pat

Change to C2.

Round 74: Rep Round 72, knitting all sts. 24 (30) sts.

Round 75: Purl all sts.

Round 76: Rep Round 72, knitting all sts. 20 (26) sts.

Change to C1.

Round 77: Rep Round 72. 16 (22) sts.

Round 78: Knit.

Size M/L only: Rep last 2 Rounds. 18 sts.

Graft together using Kitchener st.

Thumb

Place sts from holder onto needles for working in the round. Pick up and knit 3 sts in opening between hand and gusset using MC, PM. 14 (16) sts.

Work in stripe pattern alternating MC and C1 (one round of each) until thumb measures 0.75" less than desired length.

Round 1: Knit.

Round 2: *K2, k2tog, rep from * to last 2 (0) sts, k2 (0). 11 (12) sts.

Round 3: Knit.

Round 4: *K1, k2tog, rep from * to last 2 (3) sts, k2 (1), k2tog 0 (1) time. 8 (8) sts.

Round 5: Knit.

Round 6: *K2tog, rep from * to end. 4 sts.

Cut yarn, draw through rem sts, pull tight and sew in end.

Make second mitten to match the first.

Finishing

Weave in all loose yarn ends. Tack down any loose floats. Block mittens.

Chart A

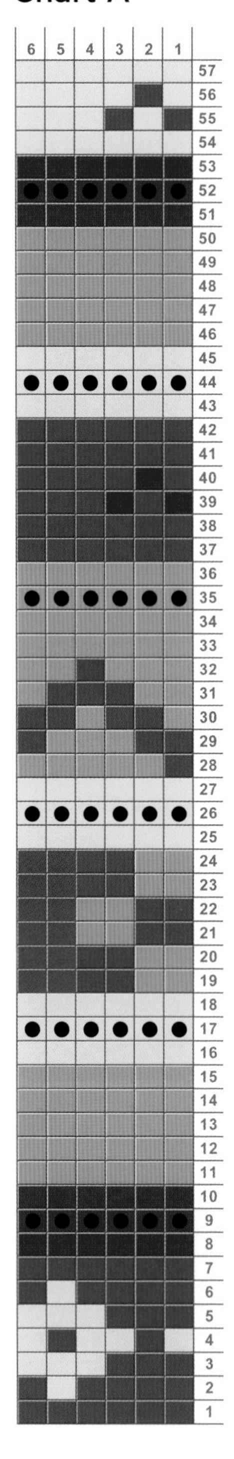

Legend

- MC
- C1
- C2
- C3
- C4
- placeholder - no stitch
- knit
- purl

Gusset Chart

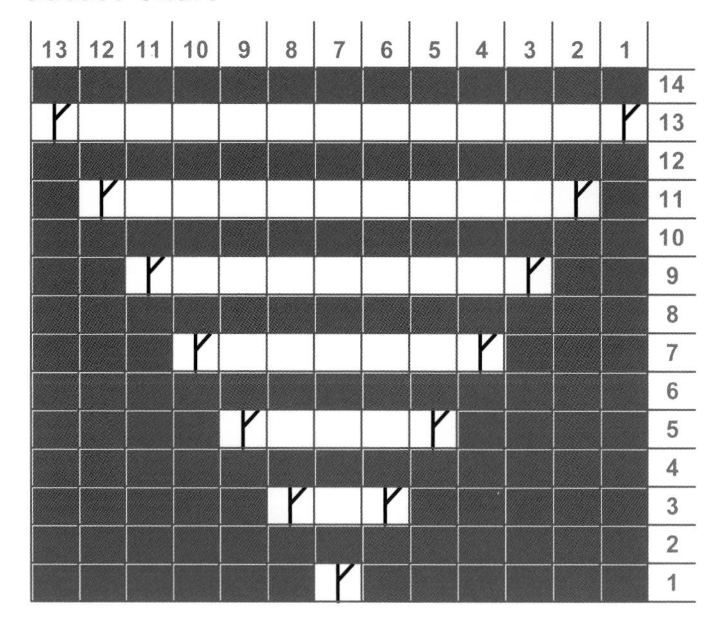

Legend

Placeholder - No stitch made

kfb
Knit into the front and back of the stitch

knit
knit stitch

BLUE SKIES OF WINTER

by Gillian Grimm

FINISHED MEASUREMENTS

32.75 (34.75, 36.75, 38.75, 40.75, 42.75, 44.5, 46.5, 49, 50.75, 52.75, 54.75, 56.75, 59, 60.75, 64.75)" finished bust measurement, buttoned; garment is meant to be worn with 1" of negative ease

YARN

Knit Picks Palette (100% Peruvian Highland Wool; 231 yards/50g):
MC Sagebrush 25549 4 (4, 5, 5, 5, 5, 6, 6, 7, 7, 7, 7, 8, 8, 8, 8) balls; C1 Spruce 25535, C2 Regal 25089, C3 Hollyberry 25539, C4 Turmeric 24251, 1 ball each; C5 Cream 23730 2 (2, 2, 2, 2, 2, 2, 2, 3, 3, 3, 3, 3, 3, 3, 3) balls.

NEEDLES

US 3 (3.25mm) 24" or longer circular needles depending on garment size plus DPN's, or size to obtain gauge

NOTIONS

Yarn Needle
Stitch Markers
Scrap Yarn or Stitch Holder
Crochet hook, slightly smaller than gauge needle
Extra US 3 (3.25mm) circular needle
Sizes 32.75-49 (50.75-64.75)", 6 (9) 0.75" buttons (number and size easily customizable)

GAUGE

24 sts and 27 rounds = 4" in stockinette stitch and stranded colorwork worked in the round, blocked. You may need to go down a needle size for colorwork, take time to check gauges.

For pattern support, contact gwgrimm@gmail.com

Blue Skies of Winter

Notes:

Blue Skies in Winter is a lightly fitted Fair Isle cardigan worked with ombre colors in the yoke and a self-faced steeked opening.

Preparing and Cutting Steek

Once the sweater is knit, form a slipknot with the MC yarn on your crochet hook. Push the hook through the knitting on the bind off row in the ditch between the first and second steek stitch. Pull a loop of yarn through; you will now have two loops on the hook. Chain one stitch, pulling it through both loops.

Looking at the first and second stitches of the steek you will see that an inverted V forms where the two meet. You'll be using the two legs that form that inverted V. Insert the hook into the legs that form the inverted V on the first row. Loop the yarn over the hook and pull it through the two stitch legs, and then through the loop remaining on the needle. Repeat, working up the sweater. Chain an additional stitch at the top to lock the yarn and break the yarn. Repeat this process on the other side of the steek, this time working from the neck down and on the legs between steek stitches 4 and 5.

Once the steek is reinforced, cut between the two legs of steek stitch 3 all the way up the sweater, using very sharp scissors. The crocheted reinforcements will turn the edge for you as you cut, pulling the cut edge in toward the inside of the cardigan.

With RS facing, in the ditch between the last pattern stitch and the first steek stitch, pick up and knit 3 stitches for every four rows plus an extra stitch at the bottom and the top. On the backside of the work, with WS facing, using spare needle pick up the backside of each stitch just knit on the front side.

On the front side, work in stockinette stitch (K on RS, P on WS) for 5 rows with the right side facing out. Break the yarn. On the back side of the same edge, knit in stockinette stitch, again for 5 rows, with the right side facing out (away from the cut stitches), so that the smooth St st face shows on the WS of the sweater. Line up the two sets of needles in parallel and knit 1 stitch from the front needle together with one stitch from the back needle.

Bind off using an i-cord bind off, adding buttonholes evenly down the front as you go when you are on the button band side.

Repeat this process with the other edge of the cardigan.

I-cord Bind Off

CO 3 sts at beginning of row. *Knit 2 of the sts, sl 3rd st k-wise. K 1 more st. 4 sts on right needle. Using left needle tip, pass slipped st over last knitted st. Sl remaining 3 sts on RH needle back to LH needle, p-wise. Snug up working yarn and rep from *.

I-cord Buttonholes

For an i-cord button band, you'll work buttonholes appropriate to your chosen buttons while at the same time, binding off this edge of the sweater. Choose how many sts you BO for the buttonhole according to how large your button are.

For smaller buttons, BO two sts per buttonhole as follows:

Work your i-cord BO off to the point where you want your first buttonhole, stopping the i-cord BO at the point when the sts have just been worked to the RH needle. Then sl the last st worked back to the needle and sl it off again k-wise, K the next stitch onto the RH needle and psso. K another stitch to the RH needle and pass the first over the second as with a standard BO. Your RH needle should now have the same number of sts you had when you started the buttonhole BO. Return them to the LH needle and continue to work the i-cord as usual until you reach the next buttonhole.

Knit Steek Stitches (KSS)

Knit the 5 steek sts. Steek sts are not included in st counts or on the charts.

DIRECTIONS

Yoke

In MC yarn, CO 5 stitches for the steek, PM, CO 97 (97, 97, 113, 113, 113, 113, 129, 129, 129, 129, 129, 145, 145, 145, 145) sts and join to work in the round. Pm to mark the beginning of the round, being careful not to twist sts.

Rounds 1-5: KSS, sm, P1, *K1, P1*. repeat between *'s until end of round.

Round 6: KSS, sm, K2, M1 *K4, M1*, repeat between *'s until 3 sts remain. K3.

24 (24, 24, 28, 28, 28, 28, 32, 32, 32, 32, 32, 36, 36, 36, 36) sts inc. 121(121, 121, 141, 141, 141, 141, 161, 161, 161, 161, 161, 181, 181, 181, 181) sts.

Round 7-10: KSS, sm, K to end of round.

Round 11: Switch to C5, but do not break MC. KSS, sm *K1, M1 (K2, M1) twice* repeat from * to * until 1 st remains, K1. 72 (72, 72, 84, 84, 84, 84, 96, 96, 96, 96, 96, 108, 108, 108, 108) sts inc. 193 (193, 193, 225, 225, 225, 225, 257, 257, 257, 257, 257, 289, 289, 289, 289) sts.

Rounds 12-32: Work Chart 1, knitting uncharted steek stitches at the beginning of each row in a checkerboard pattern using current rounds colors. Please note the final stitch in each round on both charts is a repeat of st 1 on the chart to create a mirror image on either side of the steek.

Round 33 (Inc Round) all increases are worked in C3 as follows: *K1(C4), K2(C3), M1 (C3), K1(C3), K1(C4), K1(C3), M1(C3), K3(C4), K1 (C3), M1(C3), K1(C4), K1(C3), M1(C3), K2(C3), K4(C4)*, rep from * to * to last st, K1(C4). 8 sts inc per pat rep. 48 (48, 48, 56, 56, 56, 56, 64, 64, 64, 64, 64, 72, 72, 72, 72) sts inc. 241(241, 241, 281, 281, 281, 281, 321, 321, 321, 321, 321, 361, 361, 361, 361) sts.

Rounds 34-54: Work Chart 2, knitting steek sts at the beginning of each row as established.

Round 55: Switch to MC yarn. KSS, sm, knit the following inc round for your size:

Sizes 32.75 (34.75, 36.75)": K10, M1(K13, M1)17x, K10. 18 sts inc. 259 sts.

Sizes 38.75 (40.75, 42.75, 44.5)": K8, M1(K14, M1)19x, K7. 20 sts inc. 301 sts.

Sizes 44.5 (52.75)": K3, M1(K15, M1)21x, K3. 22 sts inc. 343 sts.

Sizes 46.5 (49, 50.75)": K8, M1(K17, M1) 18x, K7. 19 sts inc. 340 sts.

Sizes 56.75 (59, 60.75)": K11, M1(K17, M1)20x, K10. 21 sts inc. 382 sts.

Size 64.75": K5, M1(K16, M1)21x, K4. 23 sts inc. 384 sts.

Round 56: KSS, sm, K to end of round.

Repeat Round 56 0 (0, 0, 0, 0, 0, 0, 2, 0, 0, 0, 0, 4, 1, 0, 0) times.

Inc Round: KSS, sm, increase 6 sts evenly across round.
Work an Inc Round a total of 3 (4, 6, 4, 5, 6, 8, 6, 8, 11, 15, 16, 12, 15, 17, 20) times. 277 (283,295, 325, 331, 337, 349, 379, 388, 406, 430, 439, 454, 472, 484, 504) sts.

Divide for Sleeves

KSS, sm, K 42 (43,45, 49, 51, 52, 55, 59, 60, 63, 66, 68, 69, 72, 74, 76) sts, sl next 54 (55, 57, 64, 64, 65, 67, 76, 75, 80, 84, 84, 90, 94, 96, 98) sts onto waste yarn for sleeve.
CO 12 (16, 18, 16, 19, 23, 24, 24, 26, 27, 25, 27, 31, 33, 34, 38) sts for underarm using the backwards loop method.

K 85(87, 91, 99, 101, 103, 105, 109, 118, 120, 130, 135, 136, 140, 144, 156) sts, sl next 54 (55, 57, 64, 64, 65, 67, 76, 75, 80, 84, 84, 90, 94, 96, 98) sts onto waste yarn for the other sleeve.
CO 12 (16, 18, 16, 19, 23, 24, 24, 26, 27, 25, 27, 31, 33, 34, 38) sts for the underarm using the backwards loop method.
K to end of round. 193 (205, 217, 229, 241, 253, 263, 275, 290, 300, 312, 325, 336, 350, 360, 384) sts on main needle.

Knit around for 1.75 (1.75, 2, 2, 2, 2.25, 2.25, 2.25, 2.5, 2.5, 2.75, 2.75, 3, 3, 3, 3)".

Waist Shaping

Set Up Round: KSS, sm, K24 (25, 26, 28, 29, 31, 32, 34, 35, 35, 38, 39, 41, 43, 44, 48) sts, pm, K48 (50, 53, 55, 59, 61, 64, 66, 70, 73, 75, 79, 82, 85, 87, 91) sts, pm, K49 (55, 59, 63, 65, 69, 71, 75, 80, 84, 86, 89, 90, 94, 98, 106), pm, K48(50, 53, 55, 59, 61, 64, 66, 70, 73, 75, 79, 82, 85, 87, 91) sts, pm, K to end of round.

Round 1 (Dec Round): KSS, sm, *K to 2 sts before next marker, K2tog, sm, K to next marker, sm, SSK*, rep from * to * once more, K to end of round. 4 sts dec.
Rounds 2-9: KSS, sm, K to end of round.
Repeat rounds 1-9 three more times then knit the Dec Round one more time. 173 (185, 197, 209, 221, 233, 243, 255, 270, 280, 292, 305, 316, 330, 340, 364) sts.
K 18 rounds in stockinette st.
Round 56: KSS, sm, *K to 1 st before next marker, M1L, K1, sm, K to next marker, sm, K1, M1R, rep from * to * once more, K to end of the round. 4 sts inc.
Rounds 57-58: KSS, sm, K to end of round.
Repeat rounds 56-58 three more times then knit the increase round one more time. 193 (205, 217, 229, 241, 253, 263, 275, 290, 300, 312, 325, 336, 350, 360, 384) sts.
On final round, inc 1 st if needed to have an odd number of sts.
Begin Hem, or work in stockinette st to 2" less than desired length.

Hem

KSS, sm, P1, *K1, P1*, repeat from * to * to end of round.
Repeat until the hem is 2" long.
BO loosely in pattern.

Sleeves

Slip held sleeve sts from waste yarn on one side and place on DPN's. Using MC, pick up
10 (15, 17, 16, 18, 19, 25, 24, 25, 26, 24, 26, 30, 34, 34, 38) sts from underarm CO and place a marker in the center of the picked up sts to mark the beginning of the round (if the number of picked up sts from underarm is an odd number, place the extra st toward the front of the sweater). 64 (70, 74, 80, 82, 84, 92, 100, 100, 106, 108, 110, 120, 128, 130, 136) sts.
Knit 7 (6, 6, 5, 5, 4, 4, 3, 3, 3, 3, 3, 3, 2, 2, 2) rounds.
On the last round, K until 2 sts before the marker. SSK, sm, K1, K2tog, K to the end of the round. K 7(6, 6, 5, 5, 4, 4, 3, 3, 3, 3, 3, 3, 2, 2, 2) rounds even. Repeat from * to * 11 (6, 0, 2, 2, 18, 10, 21, 24, 15, 18, 15, 3, 28, 30, 24) times.
On the last round, K until 2 sts before marker. SSK, sm, K1, K2tog, K to the end of the round. Knit 6 (6, 5, 5, 4, 4, 3, 3, 2, 2, 2, 2, 2, 1, 1, 1) rounds even. Repeat from * to * 1 (9, 16, 17, 17, 2, 12, 5, 1, 13, 9, 13, 29, 8, 5, 14) times. 40 (40, 42, 42, 44, 44, 48, 48, 50, 50, 54, 54, 56, 56, 60, 60) sts.
Knit until the sleeve measures 15" from the armpit, or 2" less than desired length.

On the next round, *P1, K1*, repeat from * to * to end of round.
Repeat until cuff measure 2".
BO loosely in pattern.
Repeat for second Sleeve.

Finishing

Reinforce and cut the steek, knit button band and edging band as detailed in the notes. Weave in all ends and block. Stitch buttons on to the edging band corresponding to the buttonhole on the button band.

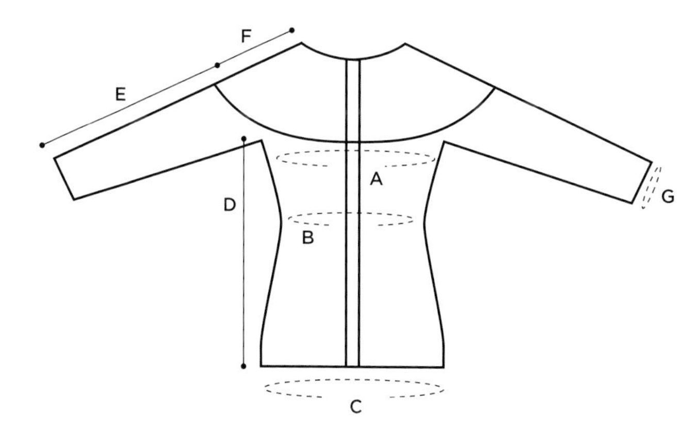

A 32.75 (34.75, 36.75, 38.75, 40.75, 42.75, 44.5, 46.5, 49, 50.75, 52.75, 54.75, 56.75, 60.75, 64.75)"
B 29.5 (31.5, 33.5, 35.5, 37.5, 39.5, 41.25, 43.25, 45.75, 47.25, 49.25, 51.5, 53.25, 55.75, 57.25, 61.25)"
C 32.75 (34.75, 36.75, 38.75, 40.75, 42.75, 44.5, 46.5, 49, 50.75, 52.75, 54.75, 56.75, 60.75, 64.75)"
D 14 (14, 14.25, 14.25, 14.5, 14.5, 14.5, 14.75, 14.75, 15, 15, 15.25, 15.25, 15.25, 15.25)"
E 17"
F 8.75 (9, 9, 9, 9, 9.25, 9.5, 9.5, 9.5, 10, 10.5, 10.5, 10.75, 10.5, 10.25, 10.75, 11)"
G 6.75 (6.75, 7, 7, 7.25, 7.25, 8, 8, 8.25, 8.25, 9, 9, 9.25, 9.25, 10, 10)"

Chart 1

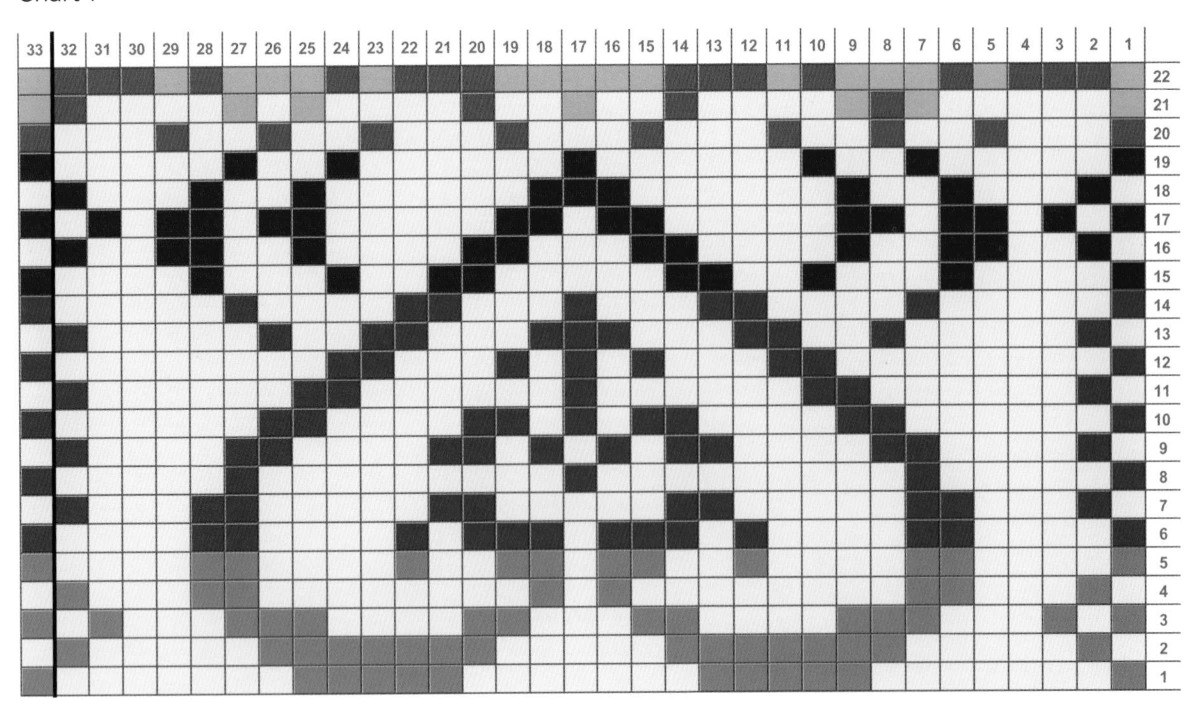

Legend

- MC
- CC1
- CC2
- CC3
- CC4
- CC5

The charts are followed from bottom to top, each row is read from right to left. Work the 32 st (Chart A) or 40 st (Chart B) pattern repeat across each round to the final st, then work st 33 (Chart A), or st 41 (Chart B). Where a color is carried across the back for 5 sts or more, twist with working yarn.

Chart 2

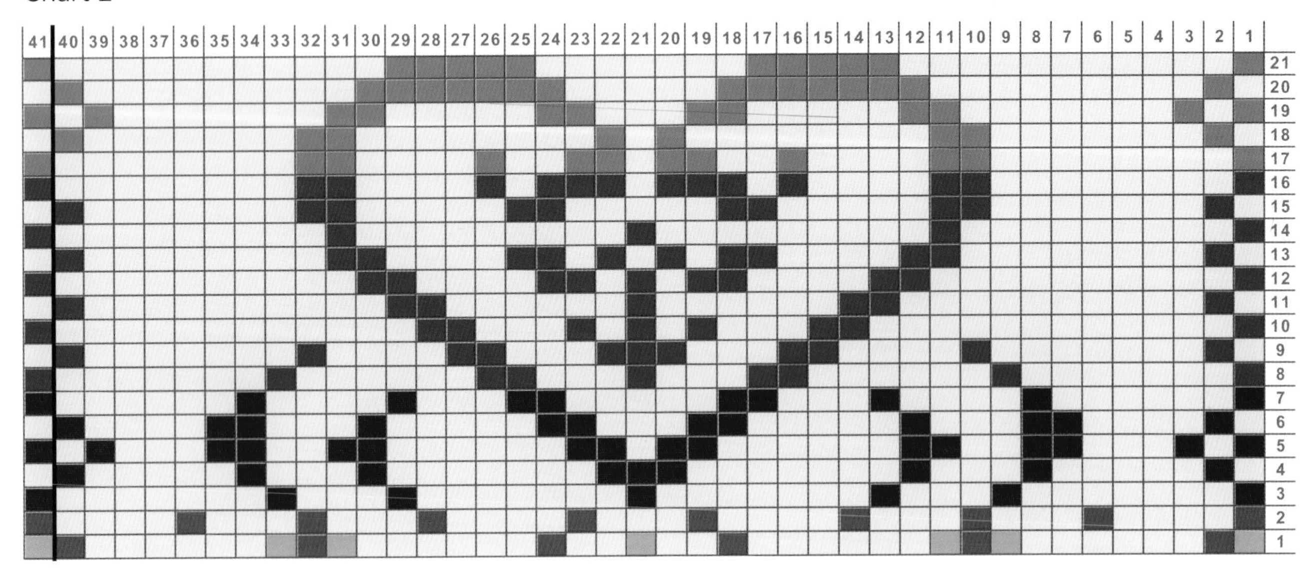

BEATITUDE CARDIGAN

by Katy Banks

FINISHED MEASUREMENTS

32 (36, 40, 44, 48, 52)" finished bust measurement, buttoned; garment is meant to be worn with 0-2" of positive ease.

YARN

Knit Picks Palette (100% Peruvian Highland Wool; 231 yards/50g):
MC Oyster Heather 24559, 5 (6, 7, 8, 9, 10) balls; CC1 Rose Hip 24556, 1 (1, 1, 1, 1, 1) balls; CC2 Hollyberry 25539, 1 (1, 1, 1, 1, 1) balls

NEEDLES

US 3 (3.25mm) 24" circular needles plus DPNs or two 24" circular needles for two circulars technique, or one 32" or longer circular needle for Magic Loop technique, or size to obtain gauge

NOTIONS

Yarn Needle
5 Stitch Markers, one being different from the others
Scrap Yarn or Stitch Holders
Crochet hook or spare circular needle and waste yarn, for provisional cast on
Sewing thread to match MC
Sewing machine for steek (or needle and thread)
12 (12, 13, 14, 14, 15) 0.5" Buttons

GAUGE

28 sts and 36 rounds = 4" in stranded St st in the round, blocked.

Beatitude Cardigan

Notes:
This cardigan is worked from the top down, in the round with a center front steek. Fair Isle motifs are placed near the middle of the seamless yoke, just above the hem, and just above the cuffs. Stitches are picked up from a provisional cast on at the neckline to work a ribbed collar.
When working the charts in the round, knit all sts and read each round from right to left.
Steek sts are not shown on the charts, or included in st counts.

Twisted Knit Stitch Rib (worked flat over a multiple of 4 sts plus 2)
Row 1 (RS): * P2, K2 tbl, repeat from * to last 2 sts, P2.
Row 2 (WS): *K2, P2 tbl, repeat from * to last 2 sts, K2.
Repeat Rows 1 and 2 for pattern.

Twisted Knit Stitch Rib (in the round over a multiple of 4 sts)
Round 1: * K2 tbl, P2, repeat from * to end of round.
Repeat this round for every round

Cable Cast On (for creating buttonholes)
Insert the right needle between the first and second sts on the left needle, draw up a loop, place the loop on the left needle. One st CO. Repeat until you have cast on the desired number of sts.

Wrap and Turn
Work until the stitch to be wrapped. If knitting: Bring yarn to the front of the work, slip next st as if to purl, return the yarn to the back; turn work and slip wrapped st onto RH needle. Continue across row. If purling: Bring yarn to the back of the work, slip next st as if to purl, return the yarn to the front; turn work and slip wrapped st onto RH needle. Continue across row.
Picking up wraps: Work to the wrapped st. If knitting, insert the RH needle under the wrap(s), then through the wrapped st k-wise. Knit the wrap(s) together with the wrapped st. If purling, slip the wrapped st p-wise onto the RH needle, and use the LH needle to lift the wrap(s) and place them on the RH needle. Slip wrap(s) and unworked st back to LH needle; purl all together through the back loop.

DIRECTIONS

Yoke

Note: Read ahead through next section. Fair Isle charted motifs begin and end in different places for each size, and are worked concurrently with yoke increases.

With circular needle and MC, using a provisional method, CO 124 (132, 140, 144, 152, 160) yoke sts. Switch to a non-provisional method and CO 6 steek stitches.
Join to work in the round, being careful not to twist stitches.

Increase Round 1: K to last 6 sts, increasing 4 (8, 19, 31, 35, 44) sts evenly across the yoke, PM, K3 (steek sts), PM (beginning of round), K3 (steek sts), PM. 128 (140, 159, 175, 187, 204) sts, plus 6 steek sts.

From here on, every round begins and ends with 3 marked steek sts. On each round, the steek should be worked in the colors that are used in that round in a checkerboard pattern (for example, all MC, alternate MC and a CC, or alternate CC1 and CC2). Use the steek to "anchor" the colors at the beginning and end of a round, running any unused colors from round to round down the center of the steek. Unless working a charted area, use MC for all instructions.

Work even until piece measures 2 (2, 2.25, 2.5, 2.5, 2.75)" from cast on.

Increase Round 2: K to marker, SM, * K2, M1, repeat from * to marker ending with K 0 (0, 1, 1, 1, 0) sts, SM, K to end; 192 (210, 238, 262, 280, 306) yoke sts, plus 6 steek sts.
Work until piece is 1 round short of being 4 (4, 4.5, 5, 5, 5.25)" from cast on, which will coincide with last round of Yoke Motif A (see At The Same Time instructions, below).

Increase Round 3: K to marker, SM, K to marker increasing 1 (1, 0, 0, 0, 1) st at the end of the yoke sts, SM, K3. 193 (211, 238, 262, 280, 307) yoke sts, plus 6 steek sts.
Increase Round 4: K to marker, SM, K1, * K3, M1, repeat from * to marker, SM, K to end. 257 (281, 317, 349, 373, 409) yoke sts, plus 6 steek sts. Yoke Motif B chart will begin on the next round.
Work even until piece is 1 round short of being 5.75 (6, 6.75, 7.25, 7.5, 7.75)" from cast on.

Increase Round 5: K to marker, SM, K to marker increasing 1 (1, 0, 1, 1, 0) st at the beginning of and 1 (1, 0, 1, 1, 0) st at the end of the yoke sts, SM, K3. 259 (283, 317, 351, 375, 409) yoke sts, plus 6 steek sts.
Increase Round 6: K to marker, * K4, M1, repeat from * to marker ending with K 3 (3, 1, 3, 3, 1) sts, SM, K to end; 323 (353, 396, 438, 468, 511) yoke sts plus 6 steek sts.
Increase Round 7: K to marker, SM, K to marker increasing 1 (1, 0, 0, 0, 0) st at the beginning of the yoke and decreasing 0 (0, 0, 0, 0, 1) st at the end of the yoke sts, SM, K3. 324 (354, 396, 438, 468, 510) yoke sts, plus 6 steek sts.

AT THE SAME TIME, work the Fair Isle motif sequence as noted below. Be sure to check and work charts as marked for your size. The motifs are placed so they are centered in the yoke and so that increases occur on solid color MC rounds. Remember that on each round, the motif is worked on the yoke sts while the steek sts should alternate between the colors used in that round.

Beginning with cast on, work 23 (23, 28, 32, 33, 36) rounds in MC.
Work rounds 1-14 of Yoke Motif A.
Work 2 rounds in MC.
Work rounds 1-15 of Yoke Motif B.
Work 3 rounds in MC.
Work rounds 1-11 of Yoke Motif C.

Continue in MC until piece measures 7.5 (8.25, 9, 9.5, 10, 10.5)" from cast on.

Separate Body and Sleeves

K to marker, SM; K 49 (54, 61, 68, 72, 79) left front sts, M1; place next 63 (68, 75, 82, 89, 96) sts on hold for left sleeve; CO 5 (7, 7, 7, 10, 10) sts, PM for underarm, CO 5 (7, 7, 7, 10, 10) sts, K across 98 (108, 123, 137, 145, 159) back sts, M1 (1, 0, 0, 0, 0), K1; place next 63 (68, 75, 82, 89, 96) sts on hold for right sleeve; CO 5 (7, 7, 7, 10, 10) sts, PM for underarm, CO 5 (7, 7, 7, 10, 10) sts; K1, M0 (0, 1, 1, 1, 1), K 49 (54, 60, 67, 71, 78) right front sts; SM, K to the end. 220 (248, 276, 304, 332, 360) sts plus 6 steek sts.

As before, every round begins and ends with 3 marked steek sts.

Body

Sizes 48 (52)" only:

Note: This adds 2" to hip, any size may incorporate them or omit them, as desired.

Work even in St st (K all rounds) until piece measures 6 (6.5)" from underarm.

Hip Increase Round: K to marker, SM, K to 1 st before underarm marker, M1, K1, SM, K1, M1, K to 1 st before underarm marker, M1, K1, SM, K1, M1, K to end. 4 sts inc.

Working evenly in St st, repeat Hip Increase Round every 2" two more times.

You should now be 10 (10.5)" from underarm, and have 344 (372) sts plus 6 steek sts.

ALL SIZES:

Work even in St st until piece measures 12 (12.75, 12.5, 14, 14.5, 15)" from underarm, or 3.75 (3.75, 4, 4, 4.25, 4.25)" shorter than desired length.

On the next round, switch to CC2 and increase 1 st at the beginning of the round; 221 (249, 277, 305, 345, 373) sts plus 6 steek sts.

Work rows 2-15 of Hem Motif Chart as marked for your size.

On the next round, switch to MC. K to the first marker, SM, decrease 3 sts evenly across body. BO all 6 steek sts (last 3 sts of this round and first 3 sts of the next round). 218 (246, 274, 302, 342, 370) sts.

Hem

Work back and forth in Twisted Knit Stitch Rib for 2 (2, 2.25, 2.25, 2.5, 2.5)". BO loosely or with the stretchy BO of your choice.

Sleeves

Return the 63 (68, 75, 82, 89, 96) held sts to the needle or place on dpns. With MC, beginning at the center of the underarm sts previously cast on for the body, pick up and K 5 (7, 7, 7, 10, 10) sts, K across held sleeve sts, pick up and K 5 (7, 7, 7, 10, 10) underarm sts, PM, and join to work in the round. 73 (82, 89, 96, 109, 116) sts on needle.

Work even in St st (K all rounds) until sleeve is 1" from underarm.

Sleeve Decreases

Decrease Round: K1, K2tog, K to last 3 sts, SSK, K1. 2 sts dec.

Continuing in St st, work a Decrease Round every 8 (10, 10, 10, 8, 8) rounds, 2 (7, 6, 3, 7, 2) times, then every 6 (8, 8, 8, 6, 6) rounds, 11 (4, 6, 11, 11, 18) times. 47 (60, 65, 68, 73, 76) sts.

Work even until sleeve measures 12 (14, 15, 16, 17, 17.5)" from underarm or about 3.75 (3.75, 4, 4, 4.25, 4.25)" shorter than desired length.

Adjustment Round: Switch to CC2 and work as follows:

Size 32": K1, M1, K to end of round. 48 sts

Size 36": [K13, K2tog] 4 times. 56 sts

Size 40": K2tog, K to end of round. 64 sts

Size 44": [K17, M1] 4 times. 72 sts

Size 48": K2tog, K to end of round. 72 sts

Size 52": [K19, M1] 4 times. 80 sts

Work rounds 2-15 of Cuff Motif Chart.

Switch to MC and work 1 round.

Cuff

Work Twisted Knit Stitch Rib in the round for 2 (2, 2.25, 2.25, 2.5, 2.5)". BO loosely or with the stretchy BO of your choice.

Repeat for other sleeve.

Collar

Carefully remove the provisional cast on and place the 124 (132, 140, 144, 152, 160) live collar sts on needle.

Raising the back of neck

With RS facing, join MC to the beginning of the back sts, starting at st number 32 (34, 36, 37, 39, 41). Work short rows as follows.

Short Row 1 (RS): K62 (66, 70, 72, 76, 80) back sts, W&T

Short Row 2 (WS): P62 (66, 70, 72, 76, 80), W&T

Short Row 3 (RS): K55 (59, 63, 65, 69, 73), W&T

Short Row 4 (WS): P48 (52, 56, 58, 62, 66), W&T

You will now be working across **all** 124 (132, 140, 144, 152, 160) collar sts.

Row 5 (RS): K to last 2 sts, working wraps together with the stitches they are wrapping, K2tog.

Row 6: P to the last 2 sts, working wraps together with the stitches they are wrapping, P2tog. 122 (130, 138, 142, 150, 158) sts.

Work back and forth in Twisted Knit Stitch Rib for 0.75".

BO loosely or with stretchy BO of your choice.

Steek

Using a sewing machine or by hand, sew closely-spaced stitches along either side of the steek center. Carefully cut between the sewing machine lines, using very sharp scissors. Fold steek to inside of piece and invisibly sew in place.

Button Band (Right Front):

Using MC and starting at the hem,with RS facing, pick up and knit 166 (174, 182, 198, 202, 210) sts along front, ending at the top of the collar.

Work back and forth in Twisted Knit Stitch Rib for 7 rows.

BO loosely.

Buttonhole Band (Left Front):

Using MC and starting at the top of the collar, with RS facing, pick up 166 (174, 182, 198, 202, 210) sts along front, ending at the hem.

Work back and forth in Twisted Knit Stitch Rib for 3 rows.

Next Row (WS, Buttonhole Row): Work 4 (6, 4, 6, 6, 4) sts in pattern, *Sl 1 st p-wise wyif. Place yarn in back and drop it. (Sl next st from left needle and psso) three times. 3 sts dec. Sl the last BO st to the left needle and turn work. Pick up working yarn again and, using Cable Cast On, CO 4 sts to left needle. Turn work. Sl 1st st wyib from the left needle and pass the extra CO st over it to close the buttonhole. Work 10 sts in pattern. Repeat from * 11 (11, 12, 13, 13, 14) more times, ending with work 6 (12, 9, 10, 14, 11) sts in pattern.

Continue working in Twisted Knit Stitch Rib for 3 more rows. BO loosely.

Finishing

Weave in ends, wash and block to diagram. Attach buttons to right button band, lining up with buttonholes on left button band.

Yoke Motif A

Legend

- MC Oyster Heather
- CC1 Rose Hip
- CC2 Hollyberry
- Size 32 and motif repeat all sizes
- Size 48"
- Sizes 40" & 44"
- Sizes 52" & 36"

Yoke Motif B
Hem and Cuff Motif

Yoke: Sizes 32, 36", 52"
Hem: Sizes 36", 44", 48"

Motif repeat and Cuff Motif all sizes

Yoke: Sizes 40", 44", 48"
Hem: Sizes 32", 40", 52"

Yoke Motif C

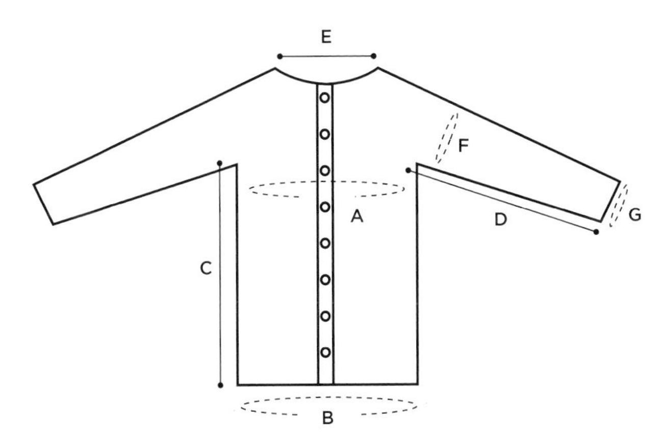

A 32 (36, 40, 44, 48, 52)"
B 32 (36, 40, 44, 50, 54)"
C 15.75 (16.25, 16.5, 18, 18.75, 19.25)"
D 15.75 (17.75, 19, 20, 21.25, 21.75)"
E 8.75 (9.5, 10, 10.25, 10.75, 11.5)"
F 10.5 (11.75, 12.75, 13.75, 15.5, 16.5)"
G 7 (8, 9, 10.25, 10.25, 11.5)"

FLOWER MEDLEY HOODIE

by Daniela Nii

FINISHED MEASUREMENTS

35.75 (40, 44.25, 48.5, 51.75, 56, 59.5, 64.5)" finished bust measurement; garment is meant to be worn with 4" of positive ease.

YARN

Knit Picks Wool of the Andes Worsted (100% Peruvian Highland Wool; 110 yards/50g): MC Spruce 23421, 9 (10, 11, 12, 13, 14, 15, 15) balls.

Knit Picks Palette (100% Peruvian Highland Wool; 231 yards/50g): C1 Opal Heather 25096, 2 balls; C2 Spruce 25535, 2 balls; C3 Turmeric 24251, 1 ball; C4 Rose Hip 24556, 1 ball; C5 Hollyberry 25539, 1 ball.

NEEDLES

US 2 (2.75mm) 16" circular needle, or size to obtain gauge in stranded St st, and two 24" circular needles for steek finishing

US 4 (3.5mm) 24" circular needle for steek finishing

US 7 (4.5mm) DPNs and 24" circular needle, or size to obtain gauge in St st

US 6 (4mm) DPNs and 24" circular needle for ribbing, or one size smaller than needle to obtain St st gauge.

NOTIONS

Crochet Hook US I/9 (5.5mm) for provisional cast-on

Optional: Crochet Hook US C/2 (2.75mm) for steek finishing

Yarn Needle

Stitch Markers

Scrap yarn or stitch holder

Sewing Machine

GAUGE

33 sts and 33 rounds = 4" in stranded St st in the round, blocked (worked in Palette)

19 sts and 28 rows = 4" in St st, blocked (worked in Wool of the Andes Worsted)

For pattern support, contact nikkisstudio@gmail.com

Flower Medley Hoodie

Notes:

This hoodie is worked in pieces and seamed. The two Fair Isle panels are worked in Palette in the round as a tube with steeks separating the front and back panel and a center steek for the front opening. The front panel creates a kangaroo pouch. The body of the hoodie is worked in Wool of the Andes Worsted in one piece back and forth from the bottom up. The sleeves are worked in Wool of the Andes Worsted in the round from the bottom up with an approximately 2.5" tall Fair Isle band above the elbow worked in Palette. The stitches for the hoodie are picked up along the neckline after the body and panels have been assembled. The hood is worked back and forth to desired length and closed with a 3-needle bind off. The Fair Isle patterns are charted only, read each chart row from right to left when working in the round, following pattern repeats as outlined in the directions.

Steek Cast On

To create a bridge (steek) across an opening on a round of one color, use the knitted cast on.

For two colors, use the long-tail cast on with one color wrapped around the thumb (usually the background color) and the other wrapped around the index finger. This enables both colors to be available at the end of the steek to continue the work.

Chain Selvage

To create a chain stitch selvage, always slip the first stitch of a row purlwise with the yarn in front and knit the last stitch of a row.

Crochet Cast On (provisional cast on)

Using a piece of scrap yarn and crochet hook, chain required number of stitches plus one or two more. Break yarn, pull tail through last loop and tie a knot in tail to remember which end to unravel from. Insert working knitting needle into first purl bump on backside of crochet chain, yarn over working yarn and pull up a loop, 1 stitch has been created. Continue making stitches through the following purl bumps until required number of stitches is on your knitting needle.

Working in Fair Isle

Yarn Dominance

For the foreground pattern to be more prominent and for a more even appearance of the Fair Isle design, be consistent in how you are holding and picking up your yarns. Always hold the foreground color of a pattern to the left of the background color, and pick up the foreground color from below the background color, the background color from above the foreground color. Inspecting the stranding on the wrong side should show the foreground color strands sitting below the background color strands.

Long Floats

To avoid snagging on the long 9-st floats on Rows 7 and 15 of Chart H, trap floats as follows: Work Rows 7 and 15 as charted, tensioning the floats so that they sit relaxed along the length of the fabric they span. On the following round, work to the location you would like to trap your long float from the last round (e.g. work to 5th st of 9-st float), insert your needle knitwise in next stitch on left needle, scoop up float from last round, and knit the float together with the stitch on needle. Float is trapped and no twisting of yarns was required.

Make 1 Increase, left slanting (M1L): Lift the horizontal thread between your needles with your left needle tip from front to back. Knit this newly lifted stitch through the back loop.

Make 1 Increase, right slanting (M1R): Lift the horizontal thread between your needles with your left needle tip from back to front. Knit this newly lifted stitch.

Left Lifted Increase (LLI): Insert your left needle from the back to the front into the back of the stitch that is two stitches below the stitch you just knit on your right needle. Knit this picked up stitch through the back loop.

Right Lifted Increase (RLI): Insert your right needle from the front to the back into the back of the stitch below the next stitch on your left needle. Knit this picked up stitch.

3-Needle Bind Off

Hold the two pieces of knitting together with the points facing to the right. Insert a third needle into the first stitch on each of the left needles knitwise, starting with the front needle. Work a knit st, pulling the loop through both of the sts you've inserted the third needle through and slipping both sts off of each needle. * Knit the next stitch the same way. You have now 2 sts on the right needle. Pass the first finished st over the second on the right needle. Repeat from * until 1 st remains on the right needle.

DIRECTIONS

Fair Isle Panels

Using the Palette yarns, the front and back Fair Isle panels are worked in the round as a Stockinette stitch tube with two 8-st steeks separating the front from the back panel. A third 8-st center steek is added for the front opening. The round begins/ends in the center of a side steek. See Fair Isle Yarn Dominance for an even Fair Isle look. See Fair Isle Long Floats for how to trap long floats without twisting yarns. Each chart row is read from right to left, when working in the round.

Lower Body

With smallest (US 2) 16" circular needle and C1, CO 180 sts. PM and join to work in the round being careful not to twist sts.

Round 1: With C1, knit first 4 sts of Row 1 of Chart A (steek sts), PM (side steek end), K82, PM (side steek beg), K8 (steek sts), PM (side steek end), K82, PM (side steek beg), K4 to end of round.
Round 2: Join C2, knit Row 2 of Chart A
Round 3: Work Row 3 of Chart A as follows: *Work first 4 steek sts, SM, work 4-st pat rep to last two sts before next marker, work last 2 sts, SM, work last 4 steek sts; rep from * once more.

Cont in pat as established, working Fair Isle charts following the pat sequence outlined in the panel diagram through Row 82. Cont to rep Rows 1-82 for panel until piece measures 15 (14.75, 14.5, 14.25, 14, 13.5, 13.5, 13)" from CO edge.

Front Opening

Next Round: Work 41 sts in pat as established (4 steek sts and 37 pat sts), BO next 8 sts in pat, cont in pat to end. 172 sts.
Next Round: Work in pat to gap, PM (center steek beg), CO 8 steek sts (see Steek Cast On), PM (center steek end), cont in pat to end. 180 sts.
Next Round: Work in pat to center steek marker, SM, work next 8 steek sts as the first 4 steek sts followed by the last 4 steek sts of the chart you are working on, SM, work in pat to end (see Front Opening Fair Isle Panel chart to help maintain pat across center 8-st steek).
Cont in pat as established until piece measures 21.5 (21.75, 22, 22.25, 22.5, 22.5, 23, 23)" from CO edge.
BO all sts in pat.

Body

Using the Wool of the Andes Worsted yarn, the body is worked in Stockinette stitch (K on RS, P on WS) in one piece, working back and forth from the bottom up from one side of the back Fair Isle panel to the other. After the kangaroo pocket height is reached, stitches for the width of the front center panel are bound off and the piece is separated for left and right sides. At armhole height, the side piece is divided into front and back pieces and worked separately up to the shoulders. The bottom ribbing will be worked after seaming.

Lower Body

With largest (US 7) circular needle and MC, CO 133 (145, 165, 185, 213, 221, 233, 257) sts using a provisional CO (see Crochet Cast On).

Set-up Row (WS): P21 (24, 29, 34, 41, 43, 46, 52) for right back, PM (right seam), P91 (97, 107, 117, 131, 135, 141, 153) for front, PM (left seam), P20 (23, 28, 33, 40, 42, 45, 51) to last st, K1 for left back.

Work in St st with a chain selvage (see Chain Selvage) for 8 (8, 8, 8, 4, 8, 8, 4) rows, ending with a WS row.

Shape Waist

Dec Row (RS): *Work to last 3 sts before marker, K2tog, K1, SM, K1, SSK; rep from * once more, work to end. 4 sts dec.
Rep Dec Row every 4th row 8 (8, 8, 8, 9, 8, 8, 8) more times. 97 (109, 129, 149, 173, 185, 197, 221) sts. 73 (79, 89, 99, 111, 117, 123, 135) front sts, 12 (15, 20, 25, 31, 34, 37, 43) back sts each side.

Note: Dividing piece into left and right sides occurs at the same time as waist to bust shaping. Read through the following section first before continuing.

Work even for 7 (7, 7, 7, 7, 3, 3, 3) rows, ending with a WS row.

Inc Row (RS): *Work to 1 st before marker, RLI, K1, SM, K1, LLI; rep from * once more, work to end. 4 sts inc.

Rep Inc row every 4th row 5 (7, 7, 7, 5, 7, 8, 8) more times. 70 (90, 110, 130, 146, 166, 182, 206) sts. 18 (23, 28, 33, 37, 42, 46, 52) sts for each front and back.

Work even until piece measures 13 (12.75, 12.5, 12.25, 12, 11.5, 11.5, 11)" from CO edge, ending with a WS row.

AT THE SAME TIME, when piece measures 6.5 (6.5, 7, 7, 7.5, 7.5, 8, 8)" from CO edge, divide piece into left and right sides on a RS row as follows:
Dividing Row (RS): Mark front center 51 sts for Fair Isle panel opening. Work in pat to marked Fair Isle sts, join a 2nd ball of yarn and BO next 51 sts, work to end.
Next Row (WS): Work to last st before gap, KF&B in last st, change to first ball of yarn, KF&B in first st on other side of gap, work to end. 1 new edge st added to each side of gap. Work these new edge sts for a Chain Selvage along gap edge.

When all the shaping is complete, there are 36 (46, 56, 66, 74, 84, 92, 104) sts each for left and right side.

Shape Armholes

Next Row (RS): Work 15 (19, 24, 27, 30, 33, 36, 39) sts, join 2nd ball of yarn and BO center 6 (8, 8, 12, 14, 18, 20, 26) sts, knit to end. 15 (19, 24, 27, 30, 33, 36, 39) sts rem on either side of BO sts.

Working each side separately, at each armhole edge (on WS rows for right side, on RS rows for left side), BO 4 sts 0 (0, 0, 0, 0, 1, 1, 1) times, then 3 sts 0 (0, 1, 1, 1, 1, 1, 2) times, then 2 sts 1 (1, 1, 1, 2, 1, 2, 2) times, and 1 st 1 (1, 1, 3, 2, 3, 3, 3) times. 12 (16, 18, 19, 21, 21, 22, 22) sts rem each side.

Work even until armhole measures 8.5 (9, 9.5, 10, 10.5, 11, 11.5, 12)", ending with a WS row. BO all sts.

Sleeve (make 2)

Note: A Fair Isle band of about 2.5" width (20 rounds) will be worked in Palette, 3" past half the sleeve length. The sleeve increases will be suspended while working the Fair Isle band and continued once the band has been completed. Feel free to substitute other pattern combinations for this band as long as they add up to about 16 rounds, plus 2 rounds before and after the patterning. Remember to hold yarns according to yarn dominance.

With ribbing DPN (US 6) and MC, loosely CO 30 (34, 40, 44, 46, 46, 48, 50) sts. PM and join to work in the round, being careful not to twist sts. Work in (K1, P1) rib for 2".

Inc Round: [K7 (8, 10, 11, 11, 7, 8, 8), M1L] 4 (4, 4, 4, 4, 6, 6, 6) times, K2 (2, 0, 0, 2, 4, 0, 2) sts. 34 (38, 44, 48, 50, 52, 54, 56) sts. Change to St st gauge DPNs (US 7). Knit 10 (10, 10, 8, 10, 8, 10, 8) rounds even.

Shape Sleeve

Note: Sleeve increases and Fair Isle Band are worked simultaneously, read through both sections before proceeding.
Inc Round: K1, M1L, knit to last st, M1R, K1. 2 sts inc.
Rep Inc Round every 5th (5th, 5th, 5th, 4th, 4th, 3rd, 3rd) round 16 (16, 15, 17, 21, 23, 28, 30) more times, changing to circular needle when desired. 68 (72, 76, 84, 94, 100, 112, 118) sts.

AT THE SAME TIME, when sleeve measures 12.5 (12.5, 12.75, 12.75, 13, 13, 13.25, 13.25)" from CO edge, make a note of your place in the sleeve inc and st count to cont with the inc after the band. Break MC.

Work Fair Isle Band

Change to smallest (US 2) needles (DPNs or circulars) and same

color in Palette as sleeve color.
Inc Round: *K1, [RLI, K1] 3 times; rep from * around.
Knit 1 round.

Beg with Row 1, work the 4-st rep of Chart J around (partial pat reps are possible depending on your st count). Work through Row 6.
Beg with Row 7, work 10-st rep of Chart H around. Work through Row 16.

Change to same color in Palette as sleeve color. Knit 2 rounds. Break all Palette yarns.

Change to largest (US 7) needles and join MC.
Dec Round: *K1, [K2tog] 3 times; rep from * around. Same st count as before Fair Isle band.

Resume sleeve Inc Rounds and when complete, knit even until sleeve measures 19 (19, 19.5, 19.5, 20, 20, 20.5, 20.5)" from CO edge.

Shape Sleeve Cap

Beg working back and forth.
BO 3 (4, 4, 6, 7, 9, 10, 13) sts, knit to end of round. 65 (68, 72, 78, 87, 91, 102, 105) sts.

Next Row (WS): BO 3 (4, 4, 6, 7, 9, 10, 13), purl to end. 62 (64, 68, 72, 80, 82, 92, 92) sts.

BO 4 sts at beg of next 2 rows 0 (0, 0, 0, 0, 1, 1, 1) times.
BO 3 sts at beg of next 2 rows 0 (0, 1, 1, 1, 1, 1, 2) times.
BO 2 sts at beg of next 2 rows 1 (1, 1, 1, 2, 1, 2, 2) times.
BO 1 st at beg of next 2 rows 1 (1, 0, 1, 2, 1, 1, 0) times. 56 (58, 58, 60, 62, 62, 68, 64) sts.

*BO 1 st at beg of next 12 (12, 32, 32, 12, 30, 12, 28) rows, then BO 2 (2, 0, 0, 2, 0, 2, 0) sts at beg of next 2 (2, 0, 0, 2, 0, 2, 0) rows. Rep from * 1 (1, 0, 0, 1, 0, 1, 0) time(s). 24 (26, 26, 28, 30, 32, 36, 36) sts.

Size 40" only:
BO 1 st at beg of next 2 rows. 24 sts.

All sizes:
BO 2 sts at beg of next 4 rows.
BO rem 16 (16, 18, 20, 22, 24, 28, 28) sts.

Finishing

Block pieces to measurements, including Fair Isle tube (flatten tube so that half of side steek sts are on each side of front/back panel = 11" wide). Weave in ends.

Reinforce Steeks: Set your sewing machine to small, straight stitches (shorter than the height of the knit sts), or use small backstitches if sewing by hand, and use regular sewing thread. Chose a different thread color than the fabric so that you can see where you have sewn. With right side facing, locate the vertical stripe pattern of your steeks. Sew on top of the 2nd st column on either side of the center line (between 4 steek sts on each side). It's better to sew on top of the v-st legs instead of the ditch in between them to maximize the piercing and therefore fixation of the yarn strands. If you feel the need, you can turn at the end and sew back up in the next st over away from the center. Keep the knit fabric flat and even while sewing. Do not pull on it as you sew or it will distort and pucker. Take a pair of sharp scissors and cut down the center of the steek, between the two center sts to separate the panels and to open the front slit—2 rectangular Fair Isle panels, the front panel with a slit at the top.

Fully Finished Steek Edges

Each steek edge will be fully encased in a steek cover and a steek lining to avoid any exposed steek edges and for a fully finished edge along the pocket openings and front slit.

Steek Cover: With second size (US 4) circular needle and C2, RS of Fair Isle panel facing, hold yarn in back of work. Insert needle from front to back between last steek st and first panel st, wrap yarn as usual around needle and bring through to front—1 st picked up. Pick up 1 st for every row along the borderline between steek and panel sts. Note: It might be easier to pick up sts using a small crochet hook. Make a note of the number of picked up sts. Change to longer US 2 circular needle.
Next Row: (WS) Purl.
Work 4 more rows in St st, ending with a WS row. Do not break yarn. Set aside.

Steek Lining: As a result from picking up sts on the RS, small horizontal bars were created on the WS. With longer US 2 circular needle and C2, WS of Fair Isle panel facing, pick up 1 st through each horizontal bar without going through fabric. At the end, pick up one extra st to match the number of picked up sts for steek cover on RS.
Next Row: (WS) Purl.
Work 4 more rows in St st. Break yarn.
Trim raw edge of steek to get an even padding inside the covered steek. Place held front steek cover sts on 2nd longer US 2 circular needle. With RS of Fair Isle panel facing, using yarn from steek cover, BO all sts using the 3-needle BO. Steam press covered steek. Repeat for rem steek edges.

Assembly: With WS of body piece facing, fold back sides lengthwise at center of armholes to front so that RS of back sides are facing. Insert back Fair Isle panel with RS facing between back sides, with top and bottom edges matching up. Using mattress stitch, sew BO edges of fully finished Fair Isle panel steek edges to back side edges. Turn piece over. With RS of body piece facing, insert front Fair Isle panel, with RS facing and slit at the top, between front sides, matching up top and bottom edges. Using mattress stitch, sew BO edges of fully finished Fair Isle panel steek edges to side front edges, leaving panel edge beyond body front side edges open for pocket opening. Measure 4 (4.5, 4.75, 5, 5.25, 5.25, 5.25, 5.25)" from each armhole edge along BO shoulder edge and sew for shoulder seam.

Hem: With ribbing needle (US 6) and MC, RS facing, pick up and knit 51 sts along bottom edge of back Fair Isle panel, unravel provisional CO and place live body sts on left needle. 184 (196, 216, 236, 264, 272, 284, 308) sts.
Next Round: K1, PM, knit to last st before picked up sts, SSK, K49, K2tog. 2 sts dec. 182 (194, 214, 234, 262, 270, 282, 306) sts.

Work in (K1, P1) rib in the round for 2".
BO loosely in pat.

Kangaroo Pocket: Sew bottom edge of front Fair Isle panel to 2nd row above hem ribbing, or higher up for a more bulging pocket. Sew body BO edge of front panel opening to WS of front Fair Isle panel.

Hood

Note: Along Fair Isle panel edge, pick up sts at a rate of about 3 sts for every 4 Fair Isle sts. Work a Chain Selvage along front edges.

With largest (US 7) circular needle and MC, RS facing, CO 5 sts using backward-loop method for hood edge facing, pick up and knit 1 st in 3-needle BO st of right slit steek cover, 3 sts along top edge of steek cover inserting needle only through front layer, 1 st in first st after steek cover, 21 (23, 25, 27, 29, 29, 29, 29) sts along right front Fair Isle BO edge, 50 (56, 58, 62, 64, 64, 66, 66) sts along BO edge of back Fair Isle panel, 22 (24, 26, 28, 30, 30, 30, 30) sts along left front Fair Isle BO edge with the last st picked up in last st before steek cover, 3 sts along left top edge of steek cover inserting needle only through front layer, 1 st in 3-needle BO st of slit steek cover, CO 5 sts using backward-loop method for hood edge facing. 112 (122, 128, 136, 142, 142, 144, 144) sts.

Next Row (WS): P4, P2tog tbl, P3, PM, purl to last 9 sts, PM, P3, P2tog, P4. 2 sts dec. 110 (120, 126, 134, 140, 140, 142, 142) sts.

Note: Work first and last stitch for a Chain Selvage.

Sizes 40 (48.5)" only:

Next Row (RS): Sl1, K3, Sl1 (for folding edge), knit to last marker, SM, K3, Sl1 (for folding edge), K4.

Next Row (WS): Sl1, purl to last st, K1.

Rep last 2 rows 1 (2) more times.

All sizes:

Dec Row: (RS) Sl1, K3, Sl1 (for folding edge), K3, SM, SSK, knit to last 2 sts before marker, K2tog, SM, K3, Sl1 (for folding edge), K4. 2 sts dec.

Next Row (WS): Sl1, purl to last st, K1.

Rep Dec row every 12th (4th, 4th, 2nd, 2nd, 2nd, 2nd, 2nd) row 2 (7, 10, 14, 17, 17, 18, 18) more times. 104 sts.

Work even in St st with Chain Selvage and slipped st for folding edge until piece measures 14" from pick-up, ending with a WS row.

Next Row (RS): Sl1, K51, fold fabric in half holding RS tog (52 sts each on front and back needle), BO all sts using 3-needle BO.

Fold hood edge lining along slipped st column to WS and sew edge to WS of hood. Sew bottom edge of hood edge lining to top edge of back steek cover. Sew bottom steek edges to front slit BO edge, overlapping slightly at center and hiding BO edge. Sew sleeves into armholes.

Optional Ties: (make 2) With largest (US 7) circular needle and MC, CO 56 sts. BO all sts. Sew to front edge of hood sts pick-up row.

Weave in all ends. If desired, block once more.

Chart A

Chart B

Chart C

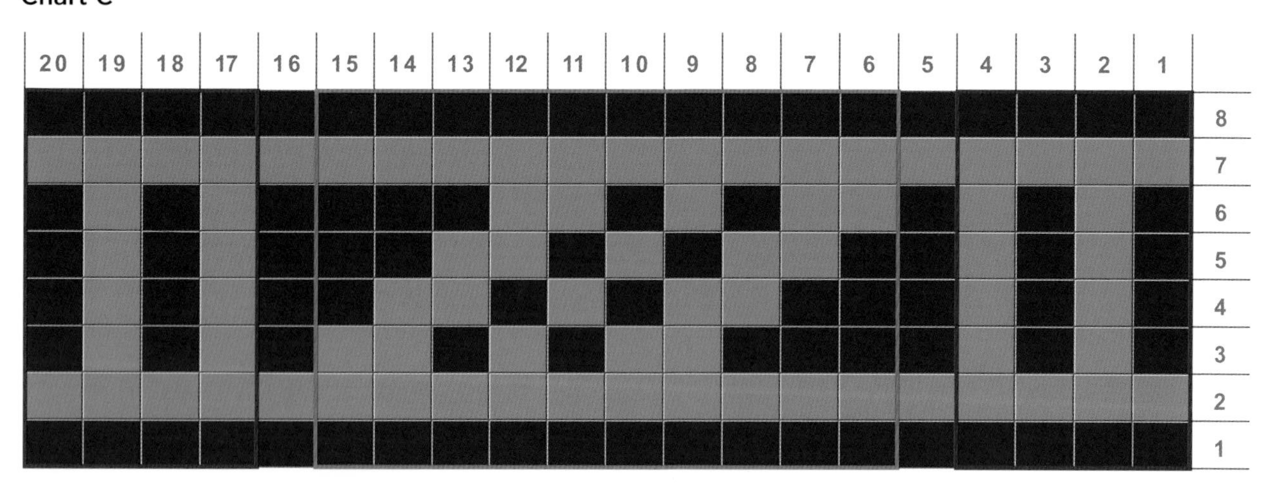

Chart D

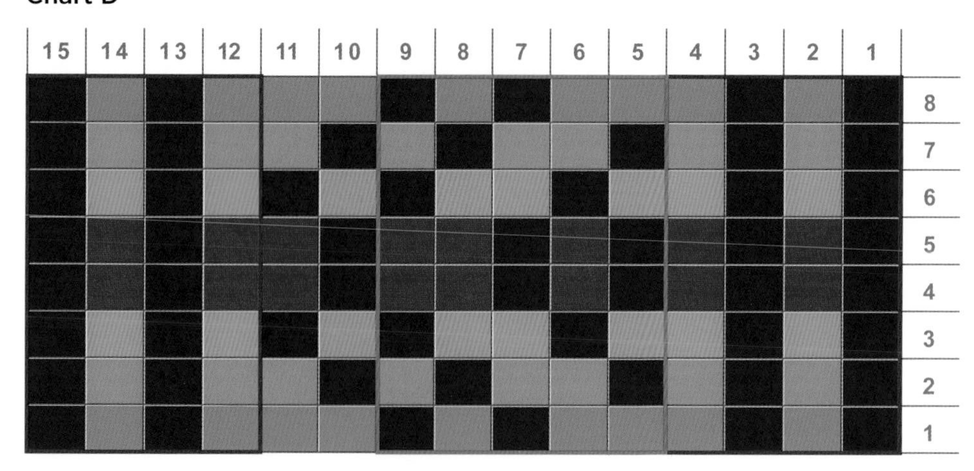

Chart E

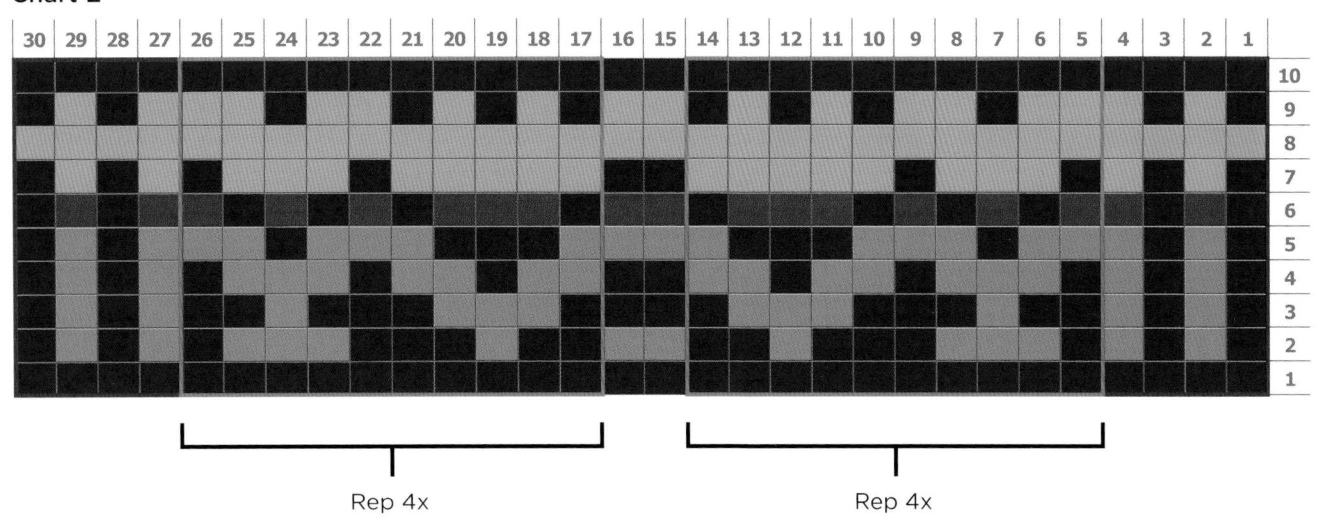

Chart F

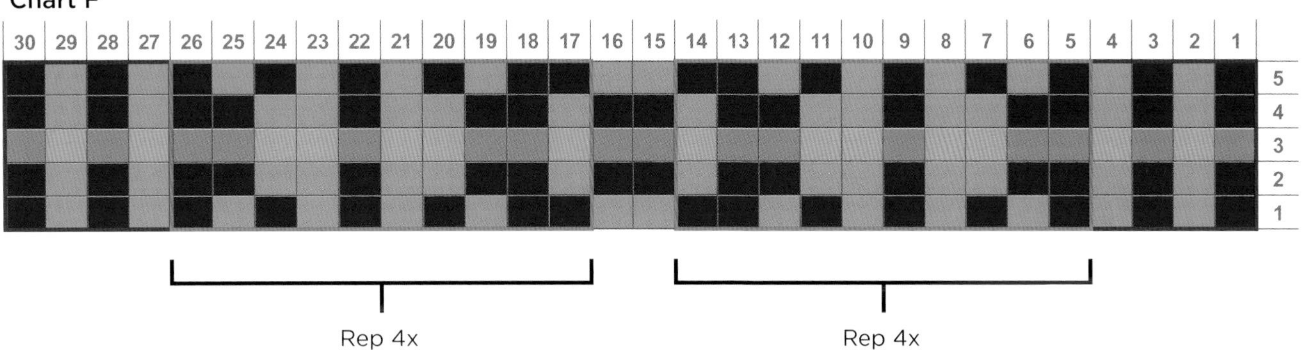

Chart G

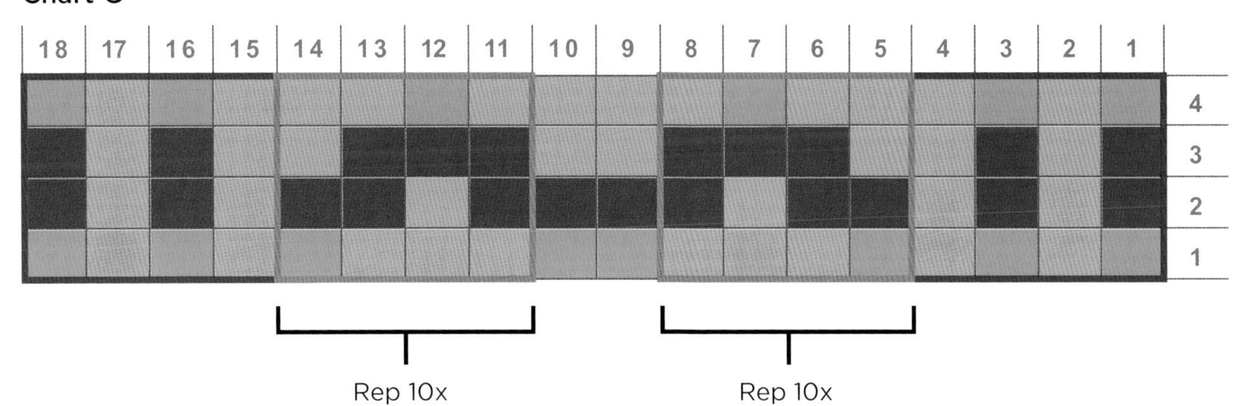

Chart H

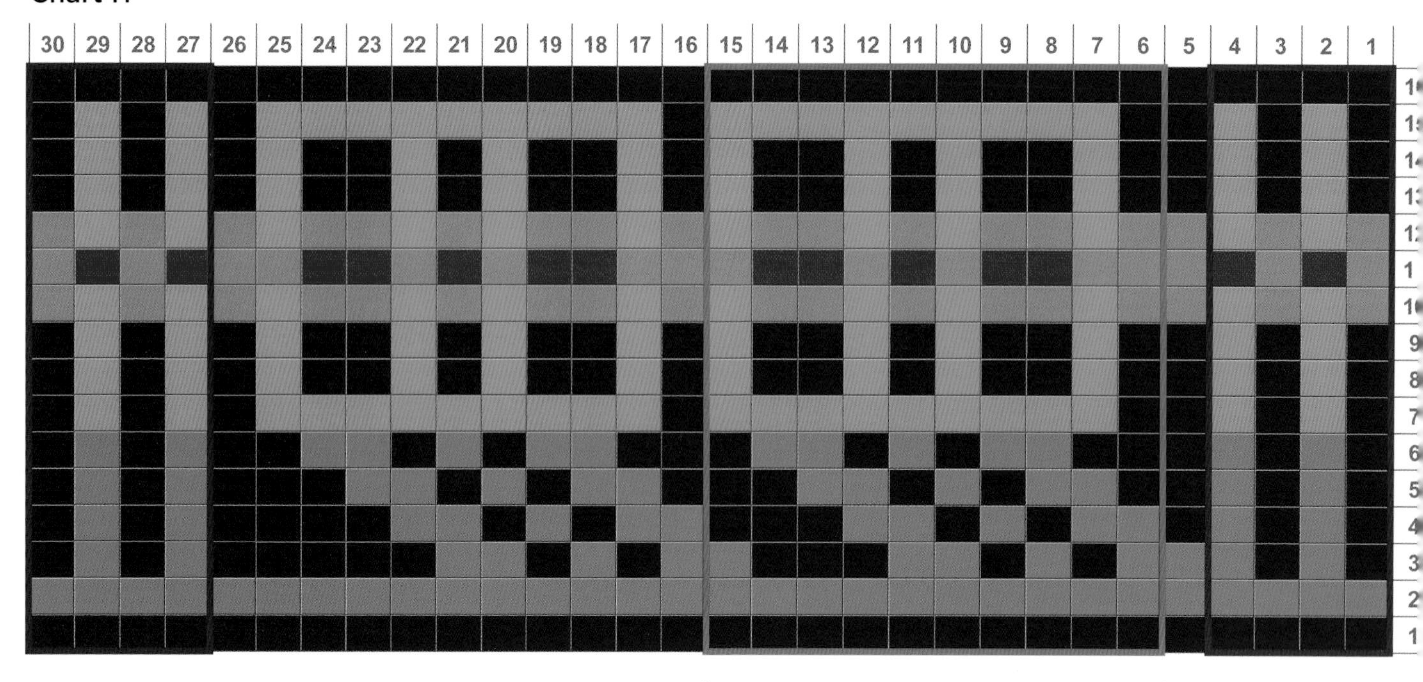

Chart I

Chart J

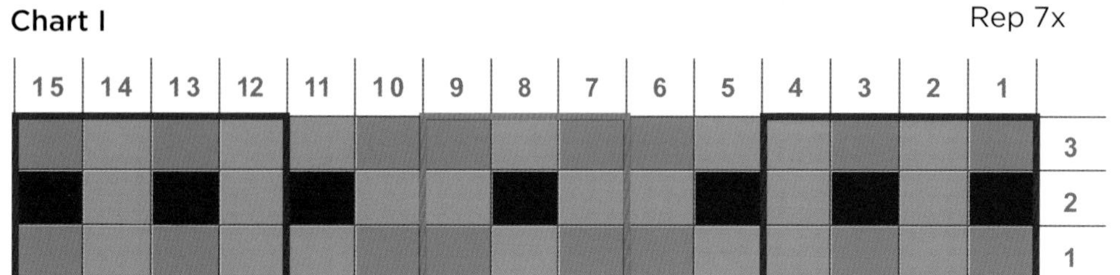

Chart K

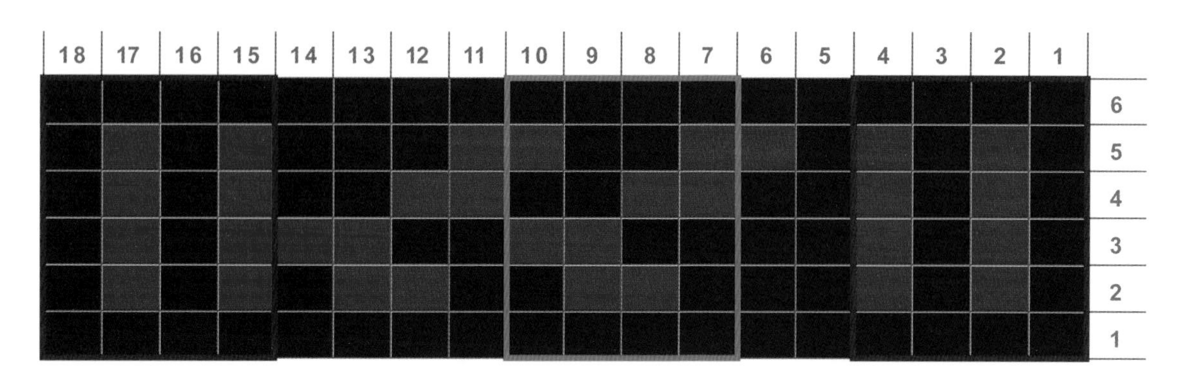

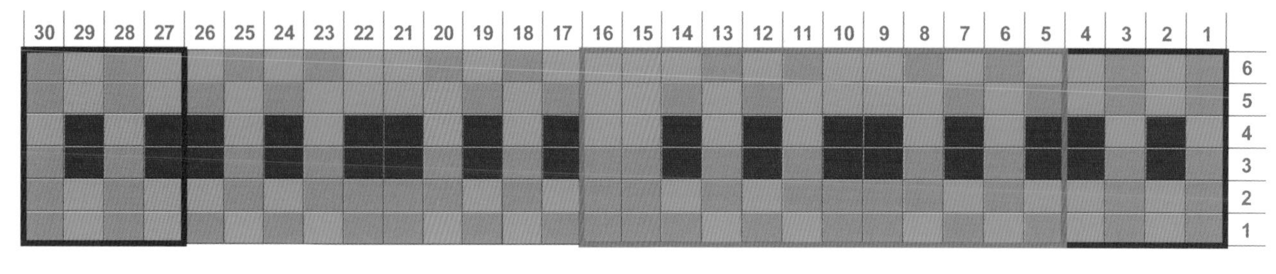

Front Opening Fair Isle Panel Chart

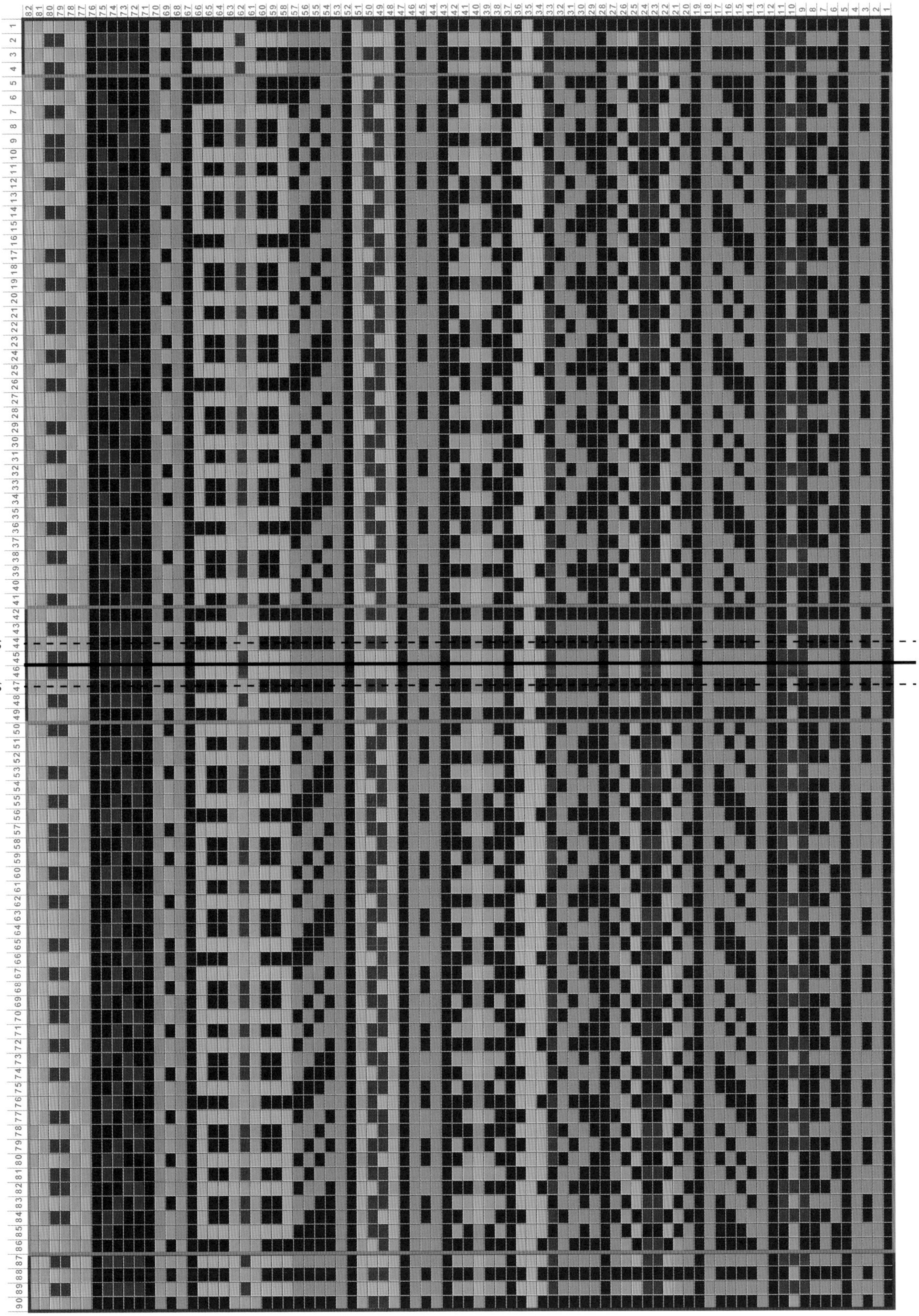

sew

cut

sew

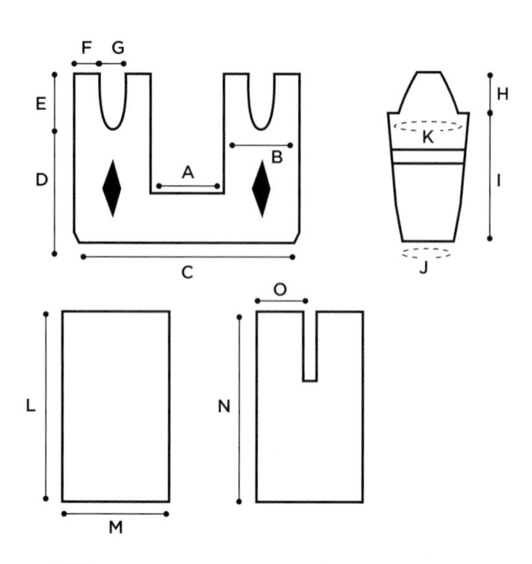

A 11"
B 7.5 (9.75, 11.75, 13.75, 15.5, 17.75, 19.25, 21.75)"
C 28 (30.5, 34.75, 39, 44.75, 46.5, 49, 54)"
D 15 (14.75, 14.5, 14.25, 14, 13.5, 13.5, 13)"
E 8.5 (9, 9.5, 10, 10.5, 11, 11.5, 12)"
F 2.5 (3.25, 3.75, 4, 4.5, 4.5, 4.75, 4.75)"
G 2.5 (3, 4.25, 5.75, 6.75, 8.75, 10, 12.5)"
H 5.5 (5.75, 6, 6.25, 6.25, 6.25, 6.25, 6.25)"
I 19 (19, 19.5, 19.5, 20, 20, 20.5, 20.5)"
J 6.25 (7, 8.5, 9.25, 9.75, 9.75, 10, 10.5)"
K 14.25 (15.25, 16, 17.75, 19.75, 21, 23.5, 24.75)"
L 21.5 (21.75, 22, 22.25, 22.5, 22.5, 23, 23)"
M 11"
N 21.5 (21.75, 22, 22.25, 22.5, 22.5, 23, 23)"
O 5"

Legend

- C1
- C2
- C3
- C4
- C5
- steek sts
- pattern repeat

Fair Isle Panel

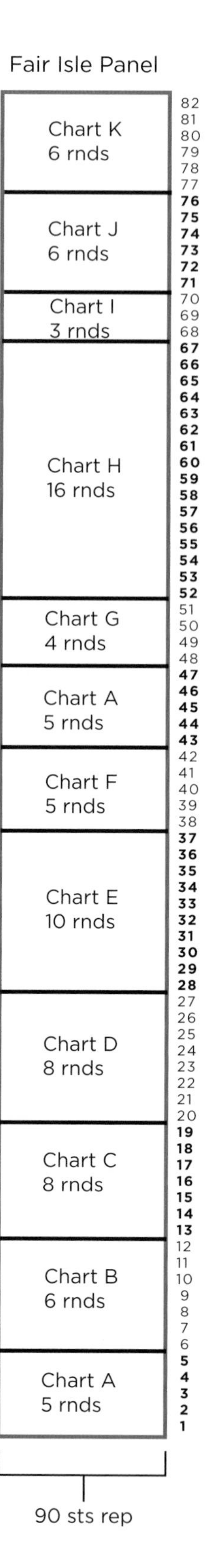

SHETLAND ROSE CARDIGAN

by Geoffrey Hunnicutt

FINISHED MEASUREMENTS

31.25 (34.75, 38.75, 42.5, 46.5, 50)" finished bust measurement when closed. Cardigan is meant to be worn with 2" of positive ease.

YARN

Knit Picks Palette (100% Peruvian Highland Wool; 231 yards/50g):
MC: Finnley 26043, 4 (5, 5, 7, 8, 9) balls;
C1: Caribbean 25095, 2 (2, 2, 3, 3, 3) balls;
C2: Regal 25089, , 2 (2, 2, 3, 3, 3) balls;
C3: Hollyberry 25539 2 (2, 2, 3, 3, 3) balls;
C4: Rose Hip 24556, 1 (1, 1, 2, 2, 2) balls.

NEEDLES

US 2 (3mm) 24" or longer circular needles depending on garment size, or size to obtain gauge

US 2 (3mm) DPNs or two 24" circular needles for two circulars technique, or one 32" or longer circular needle for Magic Loop technique.

NOTIONS

Yarn Needle
Stitch Markers
Scrap Yarn or Stitch Holder
Spare DPNs
Size E Crochet hook
7 Buttons
Sewing Needle
Thread

GAUGE

37 sts and 38 rows = 4" in stranded St st over Chart A pattern in the round, blocked

Shetland Rose Cardigan

Notes:
Shetland Rose Cardigan is knit entirely in the round from the bottom up, except for the bottom ribbing which is worked back and forth. At the beginning of the ribbing, there will be a purl row edge in the main color.

There are several steeks that the knitter will encounter. They are: center front, armholes, center neck, back neck and neckband. The neckband, buttonhole band, button band and cuffs are knit in 2x2 rib first. Next, a folding purl row is knit and lastly, a fair isle pattern is knit. The fair isle pattern is folded towards the inside of the work and sewn into place. With the neckband and button bands, the steeks are trapped inside the fold. Blocking should be done on a wooly board if at all possible.

Charts are mainly worked in the round, where each row is followed from right to left. When working flat, read RS rows from right to left, and WS rows from left to right.

2 x 2 Rib (worked flat or in the round over multiples of 4 sts)
Row 1 (RS): *K2, P2, rep from * to end of row.
Row 2 (WS): *P2, K2, rep from * to end of row.
Repeat Rows 1 and 2 for pattern when working flat.
Repeat Row 1 for every round when working in the round.

Kitchener Stitch (grafting)
Hold needles parallel, with WS's facing in and both needles pointing to the right. Perform Step 2 on the first front st, and then Step 4 on the first back st, and then continue with instructions below.
Step 1: Pull yarn needle kwise through front stitch and drop stitch from knitting needle.
Step 2: Pull yarn needle pwise through next front stitch, leave stitch on knitting needle.
Step 3: Pull yarn needle pwise through first back stitch and drop stitch from knitting needle.
Step 4: Pull yarn needle kwise through next back stitch, leave stitch on knitting needle.
Repeat steps 1 - 4 until all stitches have been grafted.

DIRECTIONS

Note: On all WS rows, carry yarn in front.

With MC, loosely CO 280 (312, 348, 384, 420, 452) sts.

Knit one row.

Row 1 (RS): K1 in MC, join C1 and use to workP2, *K2 in MC, P2 in C1, rep from * to last st, K1 in MC.
Row 2 (WS): P1 in MC, *K2 in C1, P2 in MC, rep from * to last st, P1 in MC.
Row 3: Repeat Row 1.
in Repeat the above 3 Rows, changing the contrasting color every 3 rows as follows:
Rows 4-6: C2.
Rows 7-9: C3.
Rows 10-12: C4.
Rows 13-15: C3.
Rows 16-18: C2.
Rows 19-21: C1.

Row 22 (WS): Work row in 2X2 ribbing as established in MC only.
Row 23 (RS): Knit across in MC to end.

Join in Round and Add Steek Sts
Turn work and cast on 7 stitches onto the now left hand needle using knitted cast on. Turn work so RS is facing you. Slip cast on stitches to left hand needle. The first and last stitch of the 7 are the right and left front edge stitches. Stitches for the button bands will be picked up from these stitches. The inside 5 stitches are the steek stitches. PM onto right hand needle. This is the beginning of the round.

Body

Note: The steek sts are used to anchor the contrast colors used in each round. The edge stitches are always knit in MC. For the inner 5 steek sts, alternate the MC with the contrast color used in that round in a checkerboard pattern, following the steek chart.

Setup Round:
Work steek chart, PM.

Right Front: Beginning at the 1st stitch of the chart, work Chart A over next 68 (76, 85, 96, 105, 113) sts, PM; M1 in MC, PM (this stitch is the seam stitch);
Back: Beginning at the 10th (2nd, 25th, 18th, 9th, 1st) stitch of the chart, work Chart A over next 143 (159, 177, 191, 209, 225) sts, PM; K1 in MC, PM (this stitch is a seam stitch);
Left Front: Beginning at the 30th (22nd, 13th, 2nd, 25th, 17th) stitch of the chart, work Chart A over next 68 (76, 85, 96, 105, 113) sts. 1 st inc.

Continue working in pattern as set, knitting the uncharted seam sts in MC, until sweater measures 10.5 (10.75, 10.5, 11.25, 11.75, 11.75, 12)" from bottom of work.

Begin Gussets
Note: Similar to the steek sts, the gusset sts are used to anchor contrast colors. Alternate the MC with the contrast color used in that round, following the gusset chart. Increases are worked in MC. On rounds where Chart A is worked with MC only, there will be no contrast color to knit with for the gusset pattern. For these rounds, join in C1 and knit gusset chart as indicated, breaking off C1 at the end of the round.

Rounds 1-28:
Work across Right Front in pattern as established, SM;
Work Gusset Chart, SM;
Work across the Back in pattern as established, SM;
Work Gusset Chart, SM;
Work across Left Front in pattern as established.
At end of Row 28, 328 (360, 396, 432, 468, 500) sts.

Do not knit Row 29.

Begin Armhole Steeks:
Note: You will now establish steek sts at the underarm. Work these sts according to the Steek Chart.

Work across Right Front in pattern as established, SM;

Place 21 gusset sts on a holder, remove marker;
CO 7 sts using backwards loop method, alternating MC and contrast color according to row 1 of Steek Chart, SM;
Work across the Back in pattern as established, SM;
Place 21 gusset sts on a holder, remove marker;
CO 7 sts using backwards loop method, alternating MC and contrast color according to row 1 of Steek Chart, SM;
Place 21 gusset sts on a holder, remove marker;
Work across Left Front in pattern as established. 300 (332, 368, 404, 440, 472) sts.

Continue knitting until the sweater measures 19 (19.75, 20.25, 20.5, 20.5, 21)" from the bottom of the work.

Shape Front Neck

Note: Back Neck and Front Neck Shaping occur simultaneously, read through both sections before proceeding.
On the next round, BO center 7 steek sts. Place the next 18 (19, 21, 22, 25, 27) sts on either side of the bound of steek on a holder. Cast on 7 new steek sts onto right hand needle as described above; SSK. Work in pattern until last 2 sts in round, K2tog. 262 (292, 324, 358, 388, 416) sts.

Decrease 1 st each side of center neck using K2tog and SSK as above, every round, 7 more times and then every other round 4 times. 38 (45, 52, 62, 68, 74) stitches left on each shoulder

AT THE SAME TIME, when Back measures 20 (20.75, 21.25, 21.5, 21.5, 22)" from bottom of work, AND while continuing to decrease at front neck edges, work across right front stitches and 44 (51, 58, 68, 74, 80) stitches of back shoulder. Place 55 (57, 61, 55, 61, 65) stitches on a holder for back neck. Cast on 7 steek stitches on to right hand needle. Knit to end of round.

Back Neck Decreases:

Work to 2 sts before back neck steek, K2tog. Knit steek sts, SSK. Decrease 1 st at each side of back of neck edge in this manner every round 6 times total. 38 (45, 52, 62, 68, 74) stitches on both left and right back shoulders; 152 (180, 208, 248, 272, 296) stitches total, not including steek sts.

Next Round: Keeping continuity of pattern, knit right front. Bind off armhole steek stitches. Knit right back shoulder. Bind off back neck steek stitches. Knit left back shoulder. Bind off armhole stitches. Knit left front. Bind off center neck stitches.

Shoulders

Slip the 38 (45, 52, 62, 68, 74) Right Front sts from the left hand needle to the right hand needle. The right back 38 (45, 52, 62, 68, 74) stitches are on the left needle and the right front 38 (45, 52, 62, 68, 74) stitches are on the left hand needle. Using a yarn needle and MC, graft the right back and right front shoulder stitches together using Kitchener stitch. Break off yarn. Repeat for left shoulder sts.

Neckband

Using a yarn needles and MC, whipstitch the left leg of the first steek stitch and the right leg of the second steek stitch together along the length of the steek. Repeat on the other side of the steek with the 4th and 5th steek stitches. Cut up the middle of the third steek stitch opening up the steek. Repeat this process for the back neck steek.

With RS facing, using preferred needles for working in the round, place the left front 18 (19, 21, 22, 25, 27) stiches onto needles. Next, place the 55 (57, 61, 55, 61, 65) back stitches on the needles and lastly, the remaining front 18 (19, 21, 22, 25, 27) stitches.

The right front 18 (19, 21, 22, 25, 27) stitches are on your left hand needle. Using MC, knit the 18 (19, 21, 22, 25, 27) right front stitches. Pickup 19 stitches evenly along the edge of right front and back of neck edge. Knit across back neck stitches until 2 stitches of back, K2tog. Pick up 19 stitches evenly along edge of left back and front. Knit the left front 18 (19, 21, 22, 25, 27) stitches. 128 (132, 140, 136, 148, 156) sts.

Cast on 7 steek stitches, PM. Join to work in the round.
Round 1: K1 in MC. Join C1 and P2. *K2 in MC, P2 in C1, rep from * to last st, K1 in MC.

Rounds 2-3: Work in 2x2 rib as established with MC and C1.

Repeat the above directions, changing the contrasting color as follows.

Rounds 4-5: C2.
Rounds 6-8: C3.
Rounds 9-10: C4.
Round 11: Break off contrasting color and work 2x2 rib as established in MC only.
Round 12 (Folding Edge): Purl to end in MC. Join C4.
Rounds 13-21: Work Collar/Cuff Chart.

Prepare steek as described previously and cut open steek. Fold neck band over to the inside of work along the folding edge. Pin neckband in place, catching steeks inside of the fold. Sew neckband to inside of work trapping steeks inside the neckband.

Sleeves

Prepare armhole steeks for cutting as previously described for neck steeks and cut open.

Setup Row:

Starting with left sleeve, at the left edge of the gusset, pick up 121 (125, 125, 125, 127, 127) stitches evenly around the steek edge stitches using MC. Break off yarn. Slip 21 gusset stitches from holder to right hand needle, PM on either side of gusset sts. 142 (146, 146, 146, 148, 148) sts.
Next Round: Beginning on the 23rd (19th, 19th, 19th, 17th, 17th) stitch of Row 7, work Sleeve ChartChart A to marker; SM; work Row 29 of Gusset Chart.
Next Round: Work in pattern to marker, SM; begin Reverse Gusset Chart.
Continue knitting in pattern as set until the last row of Reverse Gusset Chart. You have 3 remaining gusset stitches between the markers. These 3 stitches will be continued until the beginning of cuff.

Knit two more rounds in pattern as set. 124 (128, 128, 128, 130, 130) stitches remaining.

Shape Lower Sleeve

Work in pattern to 1 st before marker. Slip next stitch from left needle to right. Remove marker and slip stitch back to left needle. Place marker on right hand needle. K2tog with MC. Knit seam stitch in CC. Slip next stitch onto right hand needle. Remove marker. Slip stitch back onto left hand needle; SSK with MC. Place marker onto right hand needle. Work to end of round as established. 2 sts dec.

Keeping the continuity of chart pattern, decrease 1 stitch on each side of the seam stitch in this manner every 5 rounds 19 (20, 20, 20, 21, 21) more times until 84 (86, 86, 86, 86, 86) stitches remain. *Note:* Be sure to do your decreases as described above. This will hide your decreases making your work neater.

Continue knitting, keeping continuity of pattern without shaping until sleeve measures 14.5 (15, 15, 15, 15.5, 15.5)" or desired length. *Note:* It is very helpful to try on the sweater at this point to determine if the sleeve length is correct for the wearer.

Cuff

With MC, decrease 20 (18, 18, 18, 18, 18) stitches evenly across the rest of the round. 64 (68, 68, 68, 68, 68) stitches. PM. Join C1.

Round 1: *K2 in MC, P2 in C1, rep from * around.

Rounds 2-3: Work in 2x2 rib as established with MC and C1.

Repeat the above directions, changing the contrasting color as follows.

Rounds 4-6: C2.
Rounds 7-9: C3.
Rounds 10-12: C4.
Rounds 13-15: C3.
Rounds 16-18: C2.
Rounds 19-21: C1.
Round 22: Break off contrasting color and work 2x2 rib as established in MC only.
Round 23 (Folding Edge): Purl to end in MC. Join C4.
Rounds 24-45: Work Collar/Cuff Chart.
BO all sts.
Fold cuff to inside of sleeve along purl row and sew the bound off edge around the base of the cuff.

Repeat above directions for right sleeve.

Buttonhole Band

With RS facing and beginning at bottom right edge of ribbing, pick up 170 stitches in MC evenly along the edge of the ribbing, the steek edge stitch, ending at the top right edge of the neckband. You will not be cutting the steek at this time. Somewhat fewer stitches are acceptable as long as the number of stitches is a multiple of 4 plus 2.

Round 1: K1 in MC. Join C1 and work P2, *K2 in MC, P2 in C1, rep from * to last st, K1 in MC.

Row 1 (WS): Join C1. Starting at the right neck edge, *K2 in C1, P2 in MC, rep from * to end, making sure to carry yarn in front.
Row 2: Work in 2x2 corrugated rib as established.
Row 3: Break off C1, join C3 and work pattern as established to end of row.
Row 4 (Buttonhole Row, RS):
Knit in pattern 4 stitches. Work 6-stitch buttonhole as follows: Knit first stitch of buttonhole with appropriate color. With yarn in back, slip the next stitch from left to right needle. Pull second stitch on right needle over slipped stitch as if to BO. Slip another stitch from left to right needle. Again, pass the second stitch on right needle over slipped stitch. Repeat BO four more times. Return the last slipped/pass over stitch to the left needle. Turn work. Wrap the two strands of yarn around each other once. With the correct color, cast on a stitch by knitting into the stitch on the left hand needle. Draw the yarn through and place the loop onto the left had needle. Continue casting on in the correct color to follow the 2X2 rib, twisting the yarn together between each cast on stitch until you have 7 new stitches. Turn work. Slip the last cast on stitch from right hand needle to left hand needle. Knit (or purl) it together with the first stitch on the left needle. Buttonhole completed. *Continue in 2X2 rib for 20 stitches. Work buttonhole; rep from * 6 more times for a total of seven buttonholes. Continue rib until end.
Row 5 (WS): Continue working 2X2 ribbing to end of row.
Row 6-7: Break off C3, join C4 and work pattern as established to end of row.
Row 8 (RS): Break off contrasting color and work 2x2 rib as established in MC only.
Row 9 (Folding Edge): Purl to end in MC.
Join C4.
Row 10-13: Work Collar/Cuff Chart. Note: you will be knitting back and forth. Be sure to carry your yarn in front on wrong side rows
Row 14 (Buttonhole row, RS): Knit 4 stitches in pattern. Work 6 stitch buttonhole. *Knit 20 stitches in pattern. Work buttonhole; rep from * 6 more times. Continue pattern until end.
Rows 15-17: continue working Collar/Cuff Chart.

Bind off in MC, leaving enough of a tail to sew down the buttonhole band.

Button Band

Repeat the above directions for buttonhole band omitting buttonholes.

Finishing

Weave in ends. Check all places around the neck band and armholes were stitches were picked up. Close any holes with yarn needle and MC. Wash and block to diagram. Wet blocking on a wooly board is highly recommended.

When sweater is dry, cut open center front steek. You do not need to prepare the steek as noted above. When you picked up the stitches on the steek edge you secured the steek. Fold buttonhole band and button band along purl row and sew to wrong side of sweater, trapping steek inside.

With MC and crochet hook, crochet slip stitches across top of buttonhole band, around neck band and across button band to make the neck edge appear continuous.

With MC and crochet hook, crochet about 10 slip stiches on the bottom edges of both buttonhole band and button band to make them appear continuous with the adjacent cast on edges.

Sew the two layers of buttonholes together with fine yarn or thread using buttonhole or blanket stitch.

Sew buttons onto button band matching to buttonholes.

Chart A

Right front (all sizes) begin column 1

Left begin 10th (2nd, 25th, 18th, 9th, 1st) st

Back begin 30th (22nd, 13th, 2nd, 25th, 17th) st

Sleeve begin on row 7, on the 23rd (19th, 19th, 17th, 17th) st

Legend

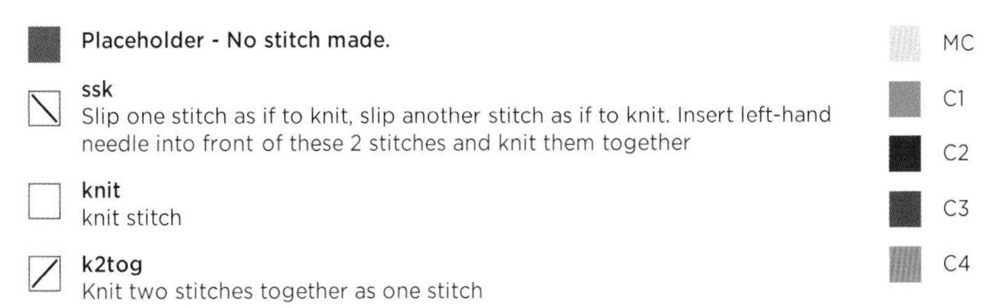

MC

C1

C2

C3

C4

Reverse Gusset

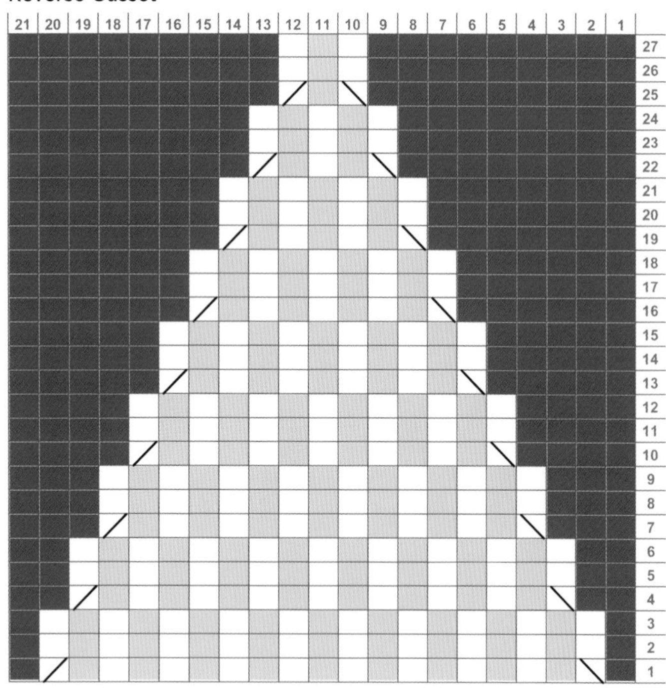

Collar and Cuff Chart

Gusset

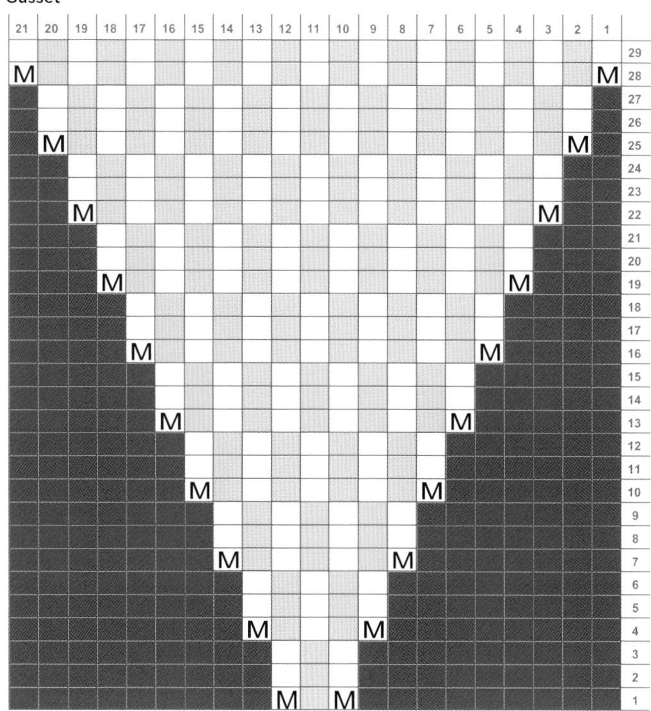

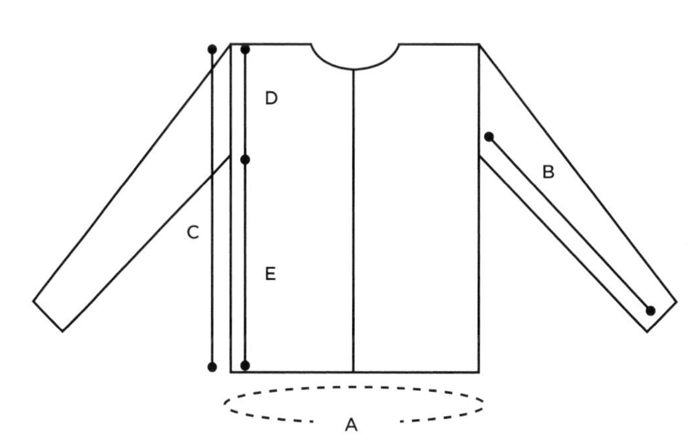

A 31.25 (34.75, 38.75, 42.5, 46.5, 50)"
B 17 (17.5, 17.5, 17.5, 18, 18)"
C 21.5 (22.25, 22.5, 23, 23, 23.5)"
D 8 (8.25, 8.25, 8.25, 8.25, 8.5)"
E 13.5 (13.5, 14.25, 14.75, 14.75, 15)"

MESMERIC CARDIGAN

by Katy Banks

FINISHED MEASUREMENTS

34.75 (38.75, 42.75, 46.75, 50.75)" finished bust measurement, buttoned; garment is meant to be worn with 2-3" of positive ease.

YARN

Knit Picks Palette (100% Peruvian Highland Wool; 231 yards/50g): MC Hollyberry 25539, 3 (4, 4, 4, 5) balls; CC1 Oyster Heather 24559, 2 (3, 3, 3, 4) balls; CC2 Regal 25089, 2 (2, 2, 2, 3) balls; CC3 Rose Hip 24556,1 (2, 2, 2, 2) balls

NEEDLES

US 3 (3.25mm) 24" circular needles plus DPNs, or longer circular needles for magic loop, or size to obtain gauge

US 2 (2.75mm) circular needles plus DPNs, or longer circular needles for magic loop, or one size smaller than size used to obtain gauge

US 1 (2.25mm) circular needles, or two sizes smaller than size used to obtain gauge

NOTIONS

Yarn Needle

9 Stitch Markers, one being different from the others

1 Removable Stitch Marker

Scrap yarn or stitch holders

Sewing machine for steek (or needle and thread)

13 (13, 14, 14, 15) 0.5" Buttons

Needle and thread for attaching buttons

GAUGES

28 sts and 36 rounds = 4" in stranded St st in the round on largest needles, blocked. For a true fit, achieving this gauge is most important.

Achieving the gauge above should yield approximately 36 sts and 42 rounds = 4" in baby cable rib in the round on smallest needles, blocked. If you achieve a baby cable gauge different than this, your final waist circumference will differ from the schematic.

For pattern support, contact KatyBanksDesigns@gmail.com

Mesmeric Cardigan

Notes:

This cardigan has a longer body length (not quite a tunic) and sleeves that come just a bit past the elbow. It is worked from the top down with a front steek. The two shoulder saddles are knit first; from this, stitches are picked up and cast on for the back and fronts. Back and front are worked separately for a bit, then sleeve sts are picked up and the whole piece is worked in the round. The finished piece is entirely filled with Fair Isle motifs except for a solid color ribbing at the waist, collar and button bands. The hem and cuffs are turned with a solid facing.
When working the charts in the round, read each round from right to left, knitting all sts. When working flat, knit RS rows reading from right to left, and purl WS rows reading from left to right.

Right Twist (RT) (worked over 2 sts)
K2tog leaving both sts on the needle, insert right needle between the 2 sts and K the first st again, sl both sts from needle.

Baby Cable Rib (worked in the round over a multiple of 4 sts plus 2)
Rounds 1-2: P2, * K2, P2, rep from * to end of round.
Round 3: P2, * RT, P2, rep from * to end of round.
Round 4: Rep Round 1.
Repeat Rounds 1-4 for pattern.

Sliding Technique (for working back and forth):
Short stretches of this project must be worked back and forth. At times, you may find that the working yarn you need is on the incorrect edge of your work. In such a case, slide the work to the other end of the needle and turn it. If you were expecting a WS row, you will work a RS row instead (and vice versa). This may save you some weaving in of ends later. In addition, for rows that involve more than two colors, you may prefer to work the first pass with two colors, slipping the stitches to be worked in the additional colors. Then slide your work to the other end of the needle, and work through the same row with additional colors, this time, slipping the already worked stitches.

Wrap and Turn
Work until the stitch to be wrapped. If knitting: Bring yarn to the front of the work, slip next st as if to purl, return the yarn to the back; turn work and slip wrapped st onto RH needle. Continue across row. If purling: Bring yarn to the back of the work, slip next st as if to purl, return the yarn to the front; turn work and slip wrapped st onto RH needle. Continue across row.
Picking up wraps: Work to the wrapped st. If knitting, insert the RH needle under the wrap(s), then through the wrapped st kwise. Knit the wrap(s) together with the wrapped st. If purling, slip the wrapped st pwise onto the RH needle, and use the LH needle to lift the wrap(s) and place them on the RH needle. Slip wrap(s) and unworked st back to LH needle; purl all together through the back loop.

DIRECTIONS

Saddles

With largest needle and MC (MC, CC2, CC2, CC2), CO 21 (21, 23, 23, 25) sts. This counts as row 1 of your chart. Work the Saddle chart for your size. After completing the last row of the Saddle chart (just before the yellow highlighted row), place all sts on scrap yarn or stitch holder.

Repeat for the other saddle.

Upper Back

Place saddles so they mirror each other with the live held sts facing out. Use largest needles and CC2. With RS facing you and beginning at the last row of one saddle, pick up and K 25 (28, 32, 34, 36) sts along the selvedge edge, PM, CO 43 (45, 47, 53, 57) sts, PM, pick up and K 25 (28, 32, 34, 36) sts along the selvedge edge of the other saddle, ending at the last row of that saddle. 93 (101, 111, 121, 129) sts on needle. This counts as row 1 of your Shoulder Short Rows chart.

Continue working the Shoulder Short Rows chart for your size. The first couple of rows look funny, but by the time you have completed the short rows, all stitches will appear correct to the motif. As you come to wrapped stitches, work the wrap together with the stitch it is wrapping. After completing the Shoulder Short Rows chart, continue to the Back Yoke chart. After completing the last row before the yellow highlighted row, place sts on scrap yarn or stitch holder.

Upper Fronts and Steek

Rotate the work so the RS is facing you and saddles are at the top. Using largest needles and CC2, beginning at the last row of one saddle, pick up and K 25 (28, 32, 34, 36) sts along the selvedge edge, PM, CO 8 sts (steek sts), PM, pick up and K 25 (28, 32, 34, 36) sts along the selvedge edge of the other saddle, ending at the last row of that saddle. This counts as row 1 of your chart. On each row, the steek sts should be worked alternating the colors that are used in that row (for example, MC and a CC, or alternate CC1 and CC2). The steek sts are not charted or included in st counts. 50 (56, 64, 68, 72) sts.

Work the Shoulder Short Rows chart for your size; note where the neck edges are outlined, the steek is worked between these lines. Neck edge increases should be worked as K1, M1R along the left neck edge and as M1L, K1 along the right neck edge. The first couple of rows look funny, but by the time you have completed the short rows, all stitches will appear correct to the motif. As you come to wrapped stitches, work the wrap together with the stitch it is wrapping. After completing the Shoulder Short Rows chart, continue to the Front Yoke chart. After completing the last row before the yellow highlighted row, follow the Yoke instructions below.

Yoke

Reposition work on needles so RS is facing you and you are ready to begin working in the middle of the steek, PM to indicate beginning of round. From here on, every round begins and ends with 4 marked steek sts. On each round, the steek sts should be worked in the colors that are used in that round, using a checkerboard pattern. Use the steek to "anchor" the colors at the beginning and end of a round, running any unused colors from round to round down the center of the steek.

Note that while working the yoke, the same row of the same

motif is used in each of the fronts, sleeves, and back. However, at the "seams" - that is, the 4 markers you place in the Joining Round - the motif will be disrupted. This is done intentionally to achieve the look of a tailored set-in sleeve.

Increases should be worked as K1, M1R at the beginning of a section of the garment and as M1L, K1 at the end of a section.

Joining Round

This round is highlighted in yellow on all charts. Begin in the middle of the steek, and rotate your work clockwise when indicated.

K to first marker (the 4 steek sts), SM;
Work the left side of the Front Yoke chart, PM;
Rotate work 90°, and begin working from the Sleeve Cap chart, pick up and K 14 (14, 15, 16, 17) sts along selvedge edge of front, K 21 (21, 23, 23, 25) held saddle sts, pick up and K 14 (14, 15, 16, 17) sts along selvedge edge of back; PM;
Rotate work 90°, work the Back Yoke chart; PM;
Rotate work 90°, repeat the Sleeve Cap chart, pick up and K 14 (14, 15, 16, 17) sts along selvedge edge of back, K 21 (21, 23, 23, 25) held saddle sts, pick up and K 14 (14, 15, 16, 17) sts along selvedge edge of front, PM;
Rotate work 90°, work the right side of the Front Yoke chart, SM;
K to the end of the round (steek sts). 267 (283, 309, 331, 353) sts plus 8 steek sts on needles.

Work the charts for your size as established.

When you have completed the last neck edge increase, place a removable marker or safety pin in that stitch (not on the needle) so you can easily locate it later.

Work through the last round before the blue highlighted row on your charts. 377 (401, 437, 477, 497) sts plus 8 steek sts on needles.

Separating Round

This round is highlighted in blue on your Front and Back Yoke charts.

K to first marker (the 4 steek sts), SM;
K 54 (60, 67, 74, 79) Left Front sts; remove marker;
Place 81 (81, 85, 91, 91) left sleeve sts on scrap yarn or stitch holder; remove marker;
CO 12 (14, 14, 14, 18) underarm sts;
K 107 (119, 133, 147, 157) back sts; remove marker;
Place 81 (81, 85, 91, 91) right sleeve sts on scrap yarn or stitch holder; remove marker;
CO 12 (14, 14, 14, 18) underarm sts;
K 54 (60, 67, 74, 79) right front sts; K to the middle of the steek to end the round.
239 (267, 295, 323, 351) sts plus 8 steek sts on needle.

You will find that the motifs now continue seamlessly around the body.

Body

Continue your Front and Back Yoke charts as established, then proceed to the Body Chart. Repeat the motifs as many times as necessary in each round.

AT THE SAME TIME, after working 31 (30, 28, 29, 27) rounds, change to the next size smaller needle (middle size) and continue to the "Belt" break in the charts.

For the "Belt," change to smallest needle and work 1 round in MC, decreasing 1 st at the end of the body sts. Then work 22 rounds in Baby Cable Rib, but keep the steek sts in St st.

Return to the middle size needle and to your charts. Note that in the first round after the "Belt" you will increase 1 st at the end of the body sts.

AT THE SAME TIME, after working 31 (36, 44, 48, 52) rounds after the "Belt," return to the largest size needle and continue through the end of your charts. Break all CCs, continue with MC only.

Hem Facing

K to marker, SM, P to marker; BO all 8 steek sts (last 4 of this round and first 4 of next round), removing markers as you come to them.
Change to middle size needles and work back and forth in St st for 20 rows.
BO all sts, leaving a long tail to sew down the hem.

Sleeve

Return 81 (81, 85, 91, 91) held sts to largest needles.
Continue the Sleeve Cap Chart, beginning with the first row after the blue line, join yarn to the middle of the CO under arm sts and pick up and K 6 (7, 7, 7, 9), K the previously held sleeve sts; pick up and K 6 (7, 7, 7, 9) more sts, ending at the center of the under arm st; PM and join to work in the round. This marker is your "seam" marker and marks the end/beginning of the round. The motifs may disrupt along this imaginary seam.
Continue through the end of the Sleeve Cap chart, then proceed to the the Sleeve Arm chart Work decreases at the beginning of a round as K1, SSK. Work decreases at the end of a round as K2tog, K1.

Cuff Facing

Continue with MC, breaking all other colors. P one round.
Switch to next size smaller needle (middle size) and K 20 rounds; remove marker and BO all sts, leaving a long tail to sew down the hem.

Repeat for other sleeve.

Steek and Hems

Machine stitch along either side of the steek center. Carefully cut between the sewing machine lines, using very sharp needles. On each side, machine stitch horizontally from the cut edge of the steek to one steek stitch from the marked last neck edge increase stitch; turn 90 degrees and continue machine stitching down 2 rows; turn 90 degrees and continue machine stitching back out to the cut edge of the steek; carefully cut between the two parallel sewing machine lines.

Fold neck edge steeks in place and invisibly sew to wrong side of garment. Fold center front steeks in place over lapping the neck edge steeks at the corner and invisibly sew to wrong side of garment.

Fold hem and cuff facings along the purled ridges and invisibly sew to the wrong side of the garment.

Collar and Button Bands

With RS facing, using smallest needle and MC, pick up and K 156 (156, 168, 168, 180) sts along right front edge, PM; pick up and K 37 (41, 41, 39, 40) sts along right front neck; pick up and K 23 (23, 26, 26, 28) sts along right saddle cast on edge; pick up and K 50 (54, 56, 64, 66) along back neck cast on edge; pick up and K 23 (23, 26, 26, 28) sts along left saddle cast on edge; pick up and K 37 (41, 41, 39, 40) sts along left front edge; PM; pick up and K 156 (156, 168, 168, 180) sts along left front edge. 170 (182, 190, 194, 202) collar edge sts, 156 (156, 168, 168, 180) band sts.
If picking up fewer or more sts seems appropriate, make sure you have a multiple of 4 sts on each button band and a multiple of 4 sts plus 2 around the collar edge.

Row 1 (WS): [K2, P2] to marker, SM, M1, P2, [K2, P2] to marker, M1, SM, [P2, K2] to the end. 2 sts inc.
Row 2 (RS): [P2, RT] to marker, SM, [P1, RT, P1] to marker, SM, [RT, P2] to the end.
Row 3: [K2, P2] to marker, SM, M1, [K1, P2, K1] to marker, M1, SM, [P2, K2] to the end. 2 sts inc.
Row 4 (Buttonhole Row): Work as established to left front, then work the buttonholes on the left front as follows. * K2, P2, K2, YO, P2tog, K2, P2, repeat from * to end of round, making 13 (13, 14, 14, 15) buttonholes.
Row 5: [K2, P2] to marker, SM, M1, K2, [P2, K2] to marker, M1, SM, [P2, K2] to the end. 2 sts inc.
Row 6: [P2, RT] to marker, SM, K1, [P2, RT] to 3 sts before marker, P2, K1, SM, [RT, P2] to the end.
Row 7: [K2, P2] to marker, SM, M1, P1, K2, [P1, K2, P1] to marker, M1, SM, [P2, K2] to the end. 2 sts inc.
Removing markers as you come to them, BO all sts in pattern loosely, binding off the M1 sts from the previous row as if they were K sts.

Finishing

Weave in ends, wash and block to diagram. Attach buttons to right button band, lining up with buttonholes on left button band.

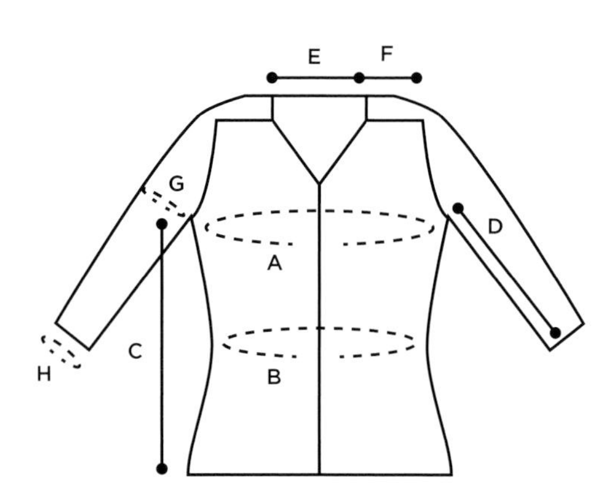

A 34.75 (38.75, 42.75, 46.75, 50.75)"
B 27.25 (30.25, 33.5, 36.5, 39.75)"
C 16.75 (17.25, 18.75, 19.75, 20.25)"
D 10 (10.5, 11, 11, 11.5)"
E 6.25 (6.5, 6.75, 7.5, 8.25)"
F 3.5 (3.75, 4.5, 5, 5)"
G 13.25 (13.5, 14.25, 15, 15.5)"
H 9.75 (11.25, 11.5, 12.5, 13)"

Saddle Chart

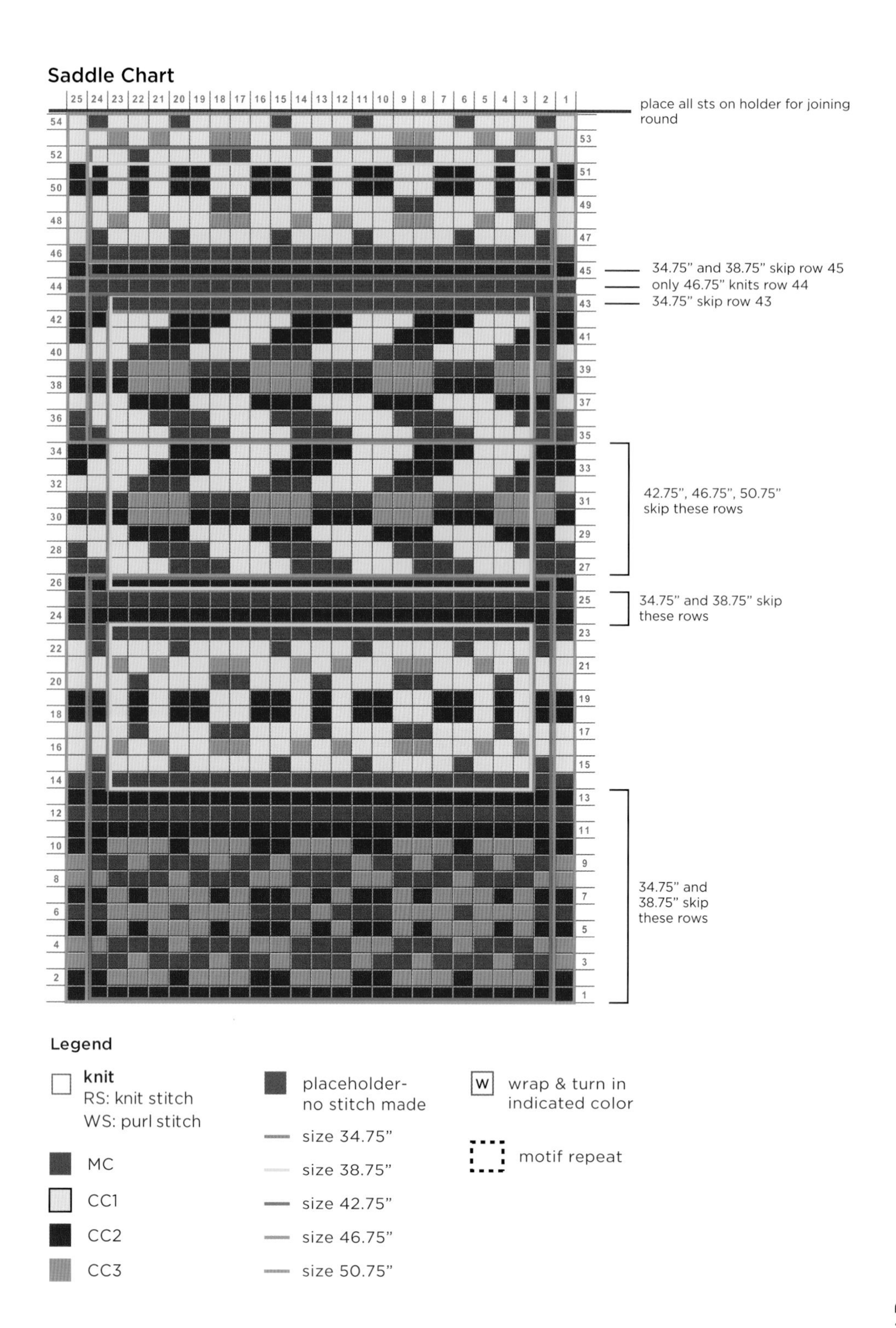

34.75" Shoulder Short Row

38.75" Shoulder Short Row

Back Yoke

G 50.75" skip rounds 22-32
F 34.75" skip rounds 22-50
E Rnd 21 is joining round for 50.75"
D Rnd 20 is joining round for 46.75"
C Rnd 19 is joining round for 42.75"
B Rnd 18 is joining round for 38.75"
A Rnd 17 is joining round for 34.75"

M Rnd 76 is separating round for 46.75"
L Rnd 75 is separating round for 42.75"
K Rnd 74 is separating round for 34.75"
J Rnd 73 is separating round for 50.75"
I Rnd 72 is separating round for 38.75"
H 38.75", 42.75", 46.75" skip rounds 33-50

Right Front Yoke

G 50.75" skip rounds 22-32
F 34.75" skip rounds 22-50
E Rnd 21 is joining round for 50.75"
D Rnd 20 is joining round for 46.75"
C Rnd 19 is joining round for 42.75"
B Rnd 18 is joining round for 38.75"
A Rnd 17 is joining round for 34.75"

M Rnd 76 is separating round for 46.75"
L Rnd 75 is separating round for 42.75"
K Rnd 74 is separating round for 34.75"
J Rnd 73 is separating round for 50.75"
I Rnd 72 is separating round for 38.75"
H 38.75", 42.75", 46.75" skip rounds 33-50

Left Front Yoke

G 50.75" skip rounds 22-32
F 34.75" skip rounds 22-50
E Rnd 21 is joining round for 50.75"
D Rnd 20 is joining round for 46.75"
C Rnd 19 is joining round for 42.75"
B Rnd 18 is joining round for 38.75"
A Rnd 17 is joining round for 34.75"

M Rnd 76 is separating round for 46.75"
L Rnd 75 is separating round for 42.75"
K Rnd 74 is separating round for 34.75"
J Rnd 73 is separating round for 50.75"
I Rnd 72 is separating round for 38.75"
H 38.75", 42.75", 46.75" skip rounds 33-50

Body

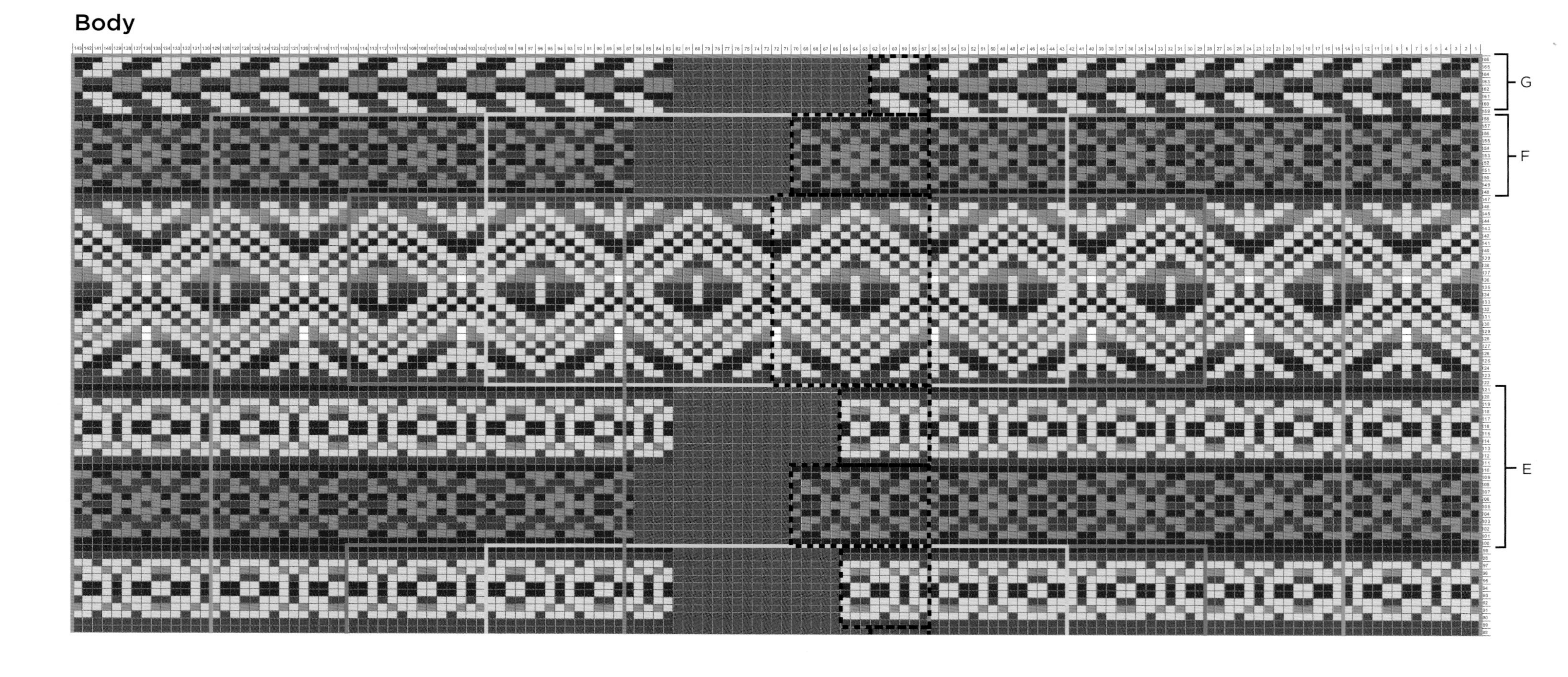

42.75" Shoulder Short Row

46.75" Shoulder Short Row

D Round 67 is marker for belt placement
C 42.75" and 50.75 skip round 66
B 46.75" and 50.75" skip rounds 55-65
A 38.75" and 42.75" skip rounds 38-45

G Rounds 159-166 for size 50.75" only
F 34.75" and 42.75" skip rounds 148-158
E 38.75" and 42.75" skip rounds 100-121

Sleeve Cap

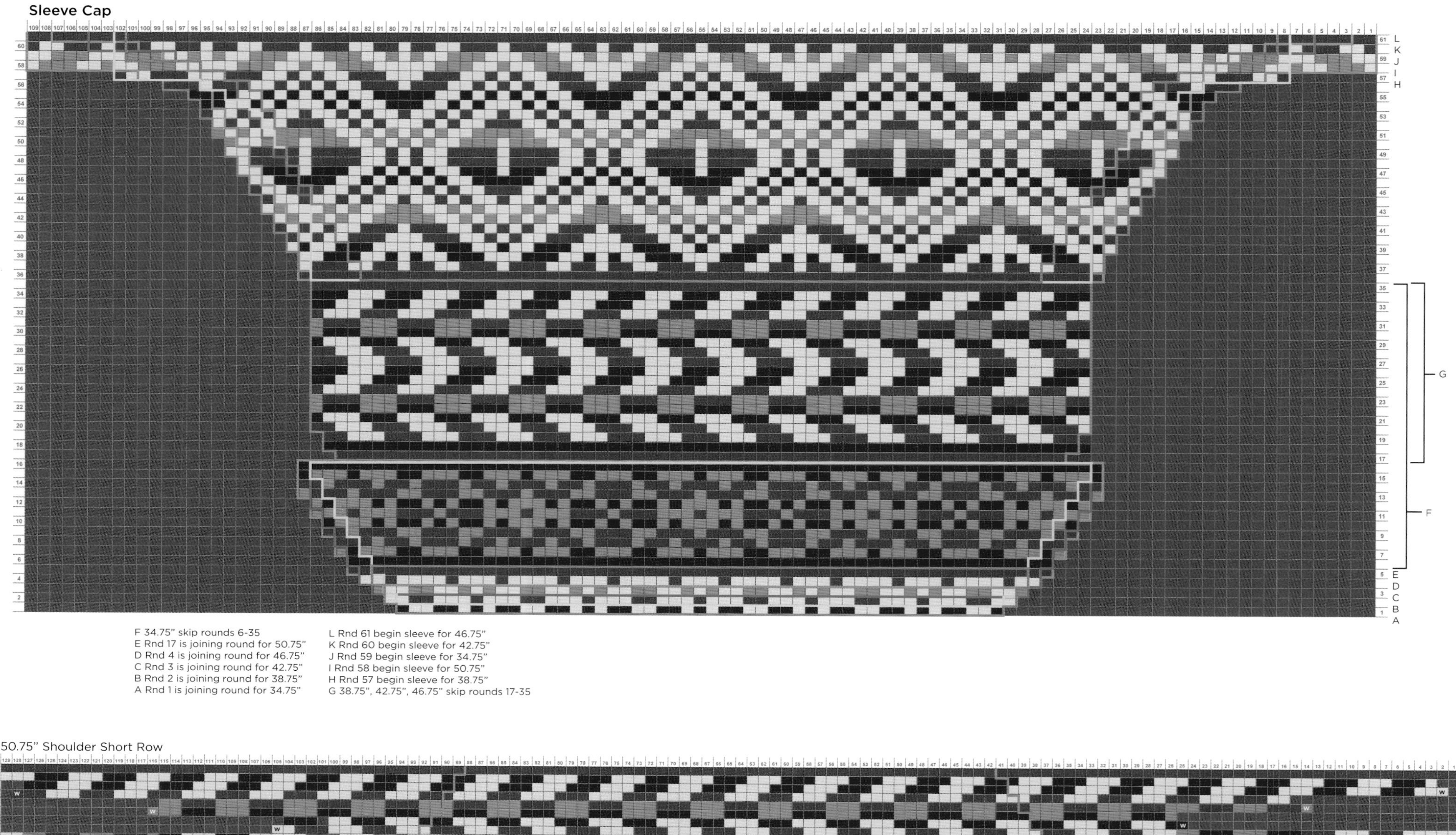

F 34.75" skip rounds 6-35
E Rnd 17 is joining round for 50.75"
D Rnd 4 is joining round for 46.75"
C Rnd 3 is joining round for 42.75"
B Rnd 2 is joining round for 38.75"
A Rnd 1 is joining round for 34.75"

L Rnd 61 begin sleeve for 46.75"
K Rnd 60 begin sleeve for 42.75"
J Rnd 59 begin sleeve for 34.75"
I Rnd 58 begin sleeve for 50.75"
H Rnd 57 begin sleeve for 38.75"
G 38.75", 42.75", 46.75" skip rounds 17-35

50.75" Shoulder Short Row

Sleeve

C 46.75", 42.75", 34.75" skip rnd 101
B 34.75" and 38.75" skip rounds 64-74
A 34.75" and 42.75" skip rounds 33-34

MULL OF KINTYRE CARDIGAN

by Anna Davis

FINISHED MEASUREMENTS

37.5 (39.25, 41.5, 43.25, 45.5, 47.25, 49.5, 51.25)" finished bust circumference; garment is meant to be worn with 3.25 - 3.5" of positive ease at bust.
28 (28, 28, 28, 28, 28, 30, 30)" finished length

YARN

Knit Picks Palette, Fingering weight (100% Peruvian Highland Wool; 231 yards/50g): MC Regal 25089, 4 (4, 4, 4, 5, 5, 5, 5) balls; C1 Cream 23730, 3 (3, 4, 4, 4, 4, 5, 5) balls; C2 Caribbean 25095, 2 (2, 3, 3, 3, 3, 4, 4) balls; C3 Hollyberry 25539, 2 (2, 2, 2, 3, 3, 3, 3) balls; C4 Turmeric 24251, 2 (2, 2, 2, 2, 2, 3, 3) balls; C5 Rose Hip 24556, 2 (2, 2, 2, 2, 2, 2, 2) balls

NEEDLES

US 3 (3.25mm) 24" or longer circular needle, or size to obtain gauge
Spare US 3 (3.25mm) circular needle, or size to obtain gauge, for Front/Neck Band

NOTIONS

Yarn Needle
Stitch Markers
Yarn Bobbins
Stitch holders
2 Snaps of desired size

GAUGE

28 sts and 32 rows = 4" in stranded Stockinette st, knit flat, blocked.

Mull of Kintyre Cardigan

Notes:

This belted, v-neck Fair Isle cardigan features a corrugated rib pattern for the hem and sleeve cuffs, front/neck band, and belt, with a modern deep, curved v-neck and modified sleeves for a more feminine fit than traditional Fair Isle garments. The cardigan is knit flat on a circular needle in stranded Stockinette stitch. The Body is worked in one piece to armholes and then divided for Right Front, Back, and Left Front, then working each section individually to the shoulders. V-neck bind offs begin before armhole bind offs and then both are worked simultaneously. The use of yarn bobbins and spit-splicing yarn ends are recommended. When knitting Fair Isle patterns, keep yarn tension fairly loose, and remember to be consistent carrying the main color in use, either under, or over, the contrast color(s) across the entire row. This helps prevent "bubbling" of the fabric and maintains consistent color dominance throughout the entire garment. Charts are provided for Right Front, Back, and Left Front indicating v-neck decreases and armhole bind offs, vertical pattern repeats, and the extra stitch at hem rib. A Sleeve chart is also provided indicating increases (see Special Instructions) and sleeve cap bind offs, as well as vertical pattern repeats. Two additional charts include: a Fair Isle pattern repeats chart, including a charts key for all the charts included, and a Corrugated Ribs charts for the Belt and Front/Neck Band. When working charts, follow from the bottom up, RS (odd numbered) rows from right to left, and WS (even numbered) rows from left to right.

Corrugated Rib Pattern (worked flat, over an odd number of sts)
Beginning with MC, knit one stitch. *Change to CC. Bring yarn to front and purl next stitch. Return the CC yarn to the back of work. Change to MC and knit next stitch.* Rep from * to *.
Row 1 (RS): *K1, P1, rep from * to last st, K1.
Row 2 (WS): *P1, K1, rep from * to last st, P1.
Repeat Rows 1 and 2 for pattern.

Corrugated Rib Pattern (worked flat, over an even number of sts)
Working with two colors as described above,
All Rows: *K1, P1, rep from * to end.

M1R/M1L: Sleeve Increases (worked in Stranded Fair Isle pattern, with selvedge)
This increasing technique prevents disruption of charted patterns, and creates a neat selvedge. Use M1R at right edge of sleeve, and M1L at left edge of sleeve.
M1R: K1. Lift the correct color strand for the next stitch color in charted pattern, and place new stitch on LH needle. Knit this stitch through the front loop.
M1L: Work across row to last two stitches. Lift the correct color strand for the next stitch color in charted pattern, and place new stitch on LH needle. Knit this stitch through the back loop. K1.

Stretchy Bind Off
This makes a stretchy, but sturdy bind off that leaves a neat and tidy edge. Use this method for all bind offs except Front V-Neck and Armholes.
K1, *K1 and pull up, but do not pull sts off LH needle. With LH needle, slip first knit stitch over second knit stitch on RH needle. Pull stitches off LH needle. * Rep from * to *. At end of row, pull final BO stitch up, cut yarn, and slip end of yarn through loop. Pull to secure end.

Sloped Bind Off for Front V-Neck and Armholes
This makes a smooth curve preventing the "stair steps" formed with a regular bind-off.
Work row to last stitch, but do not work this stitch. Turn work. The unworked stitch becomes the first stitch on RH needle. Keeping yarn in back of work, slip the first stitch on the LH needle purlwise, then bind off the unworked stitch by lifting it over the slipped stitch and off the needle.

Cable Cast On
This makes a neat, yet flexible cast on edge.
Place slip knot on LH needle. Knit one stitch. There are now two stitches on LH needle. *Insert RH needle between the two stitches on LH needle, wrap yarn as usual and bring new stitch up through the middle of previous two stitches. Transfer the newly created stitch onto the LH needle.* Rep from * to * to the required number of stitches.

Spit-Splicing Yarn (Traditional)
This helps prevent yarn waste and cuts down on the amount of yarn ends to be woven in when finishing garment.
Separate yarn strands at end of yarn in use and new yarn to be joined. Rub slightly to loosen fibers. Hold ends together intertwining all unraveled strands. Wet this join with mouth or water. Rub the joined yarn ends together repeatedly in palm of hand. Repeat until join is smooth, dry, and a similar thickness to yarn used throughout.

Reading Charts
The Stranded Fair Isle Patterns are worked flat. The charts are worked from the bottom up. On RS (odd numbered) rows, knit the stitches in the charted color(s). On WS (even-numbered) rows, purl the stitches in the charted color(s). Make sure to begin and end each chart on the correct stitch column for your size, following the colored lines.

DIRECTIONS

Body

Entire garment width is worked flat from the bottom up in one piece to armholes and then divided into Right Front, Back, and Left Front to be worked to Shoulders.

Hem
With MC, using the Cable cast on method, CO 249 (261, 277, 289, 305, 317, 333, 345) sts.

Begin following charts for Right Front, Back and Left Front, working from the bottom up and reading RS (odd numbered) rows from Right Front to Back to Left Front and WS (even numbered) rows from Left Front to Back to Right Front.

Beg with RS row, work Rows 1-16 in Corrugated Rib pattern (over an odd number of sts).

With MC only, work next two chart rows as set up rows.
Row 17 (RS, Dec row): K 124 (130, 138, 144, 152, 158, 166, 172) sts.

K2togtbl, K 124 (130, 138, 144, 152, 158, 166, 172) sts. 1 st dec.
Row 18 (WS): Purl.

The remainder of the Body is worked in Stranded Fair Isle pattern, worked flat. On the next row, you will place markers to denote Right Front/Back/Left Front.

Row 19 (RS): K 62 (65, 69, 72, 76, 79, 83, 86) sts for Right Front, PM, K 124 (130, 138, 144, 152, 158, 166, 172) sts for Back, PM, K 62 (65, 69, 72, 76, 79, 83, 86) sts for Left Front.

Continue in pattern as established, slipping side markers on every row, and work even in Stranded Fair Isle pattern until garment length measures 16 (16, 16, 16, 16, 16, 18, 18)" from cast on edge, ending with a WS row.

V-Neck Shaping

Note: V-neck shaping is worked on the RS for Right Front, and on the WS for Left Front at the same time, and begins before Armhole bind offs begin, and then both Right Front and Left Front V-necks shaping and Armholes shaping are all worked simultaneously; please read through to end of Armhole Shaping instructions before proceeding. Remember to check garment length, slipping armhole markers on every row to ensure accurate armhole placements.

V-Neck Shaping/Right Front

Using Sloped Bind Off, BO sts for V-neck shaping at the neck edge on RS rows as follows:
BO 2 sts on every RS row, 8 times; then BO 1 st on every 6th (6th, 4th, 4th, 4th, 4th, 4th, 4th) row, 8 (12, 3, 6, 9, 9, 12, 12) times; then BO 1 st on every 8th (8th, 6th, 6th, 6th, 6th, 6th, 6th) row, 3 (0, 10, 8, 6, 6, 4, 4) times.
Work WS rows as: Work in pattern to last st, Sl1.
27 (28, 29, 30, 31, 31, 32, 32) sts bound off at neck edge.

Continuing in Stranded Fair Isle pattern, work even until garment length measures 28 (28, 28, 28, 28, 28, 30, 30)" from cast on edge or 7 (7.25, 7.5, 7.75, 8, 8.25, 8.5, 8.5)" from armhole, ending on a WS row. Make a note of the chart row worked.

Next row (RS): Loosely BO the 26 (28, 29, 30, 31, 31, 30, 31) sts for Right Front Shoulder.

V-Neck Shaping/Left Front

Using Sloped Bind Off, BO sts for V-neck shaping at the neck edge on WS rows as follows:
BO 2 sts on every WS row, 8 times; then BO 1 st on every 6th (6th, 4th, 4th, 4th, 4th, 4th, 4th) row, 8 (12, 3, 6, 9, 9, 12, 12) times; then BO 1 st on every 8th (8th, 6th, 6th, 6th, 6th, 6th, 6th) row, 3 (0, 10, 8, 6, 6, 4, 4) times, ending on WS row.
Work RS rows as: Work in pattern to last st, Sl1.
27 (28, 29, 30, 31, 31, 32, 32) sts bound off at neck edge.

Continuing in Stranded Fair Isle pattern, work even until garment length measures 28 (28, 28, 28, 28, 28, 30, 30)" from cast on edge or 7 (7.25, 7.5, 7.75, 8, 8.25, 8.5, 8.5)" from armhole, ending on a WS row, and making sure to end on the same chart row as Right Front.

Next row (RS): Loosely BO rem 26 (28, 29, 30, 31, 31, 30, 31) sts for Left Front Shoulder.

Armhole Shaping

AT SAME TIME as V-neck Shaping, begin Armhole shaping when garment length measures 21 (20.75, 20.5, 20.25, 20, 19.75, 21.5, 21.5)" from cast on edge, ending with a WS row.

Divide Right Front/Back/Left Front at Armhole

Next Row (RS): Work across Right Front sts, working V-neck shaping, to 4 (4, 4, 4, 4, 7, 7, 7) sts before side seam marker, BO next 8 (8, 8, 8, 8, 14, 14, 14) sts removing marker, place the Right Front sts just worked on holder; work across Back sts to 4 (4, 4, 4, 4, 7, 7, 7) sts before next side seam marker, BO next 8 (8, 8, 8, 8, 14, 14, 14) sts removing marker, place the Back sts just worked on a separate holder; work across Left Front to last st, Sl1.

Armhole Shaping/Left Front

Working across Left Front sts only, continue Left Front V-neck shaping on WS rows, and begin working Armhole shaping at the armhole edge on RS rows, using Sloped Bind Off for all shaping. BO 2 (2, 2, 2, 3, 2, 2, 3) sts on next RS row; then BO 2 sts every RS row, 0 (0, 1, 1, 1, 1, 2, 2) time(s); then BO 1 st every RS row, 3 (3, 3, 4, 5, 6, 8, 9) times. 5 (5, 5, 7, 8, 10, 10, 14, 16) sts bound off at armhole edge.

Continue working even at the armhole edge, and bind off as described in the V-Neck Shaping/Left Front section.

Armhole Shaping/Back

Back Right Armhole shaping is worked on every WS row, and Back Left Armhole shaping is worked on every RS row, using Sloped Bind Off for all shaping.

Replace held Back sts on the needle. With WS facing, join new yarn. Beg with a WS row, work Left and Right Back armhole bind offs on every row (RS & WS), at both Left and Right armhole edges:
BO 2 (2, 2, 2, 3, 2, 2, 3) sts on every row 1 time; then BO 2 sts on every row 0 (0, 1, 1, 1, 1, 2, 2) time(s); then BO 1 st on every row 3 (3, 3, 4, 5, 6, 8, 9) times. 5 (5, 7, 8, 10, 10, 14, 16) sts BO at each armhole edge. 106 (112, 116, 120, 124, 124, 124, 126) sts on needle.

Continue working even until each armholes measures 6.75 (7, 7.25, 7.5, 7.75, 8, 8.25, 8.25)" from armhole, ending on a WS row. Make sure to end 3 rows before the chart row noted on the Right Front.

Back Neck

Next Row (RS): K 26 (28, 29, 30, 31, 31, 30, 31) sts for Right Back Shoulder, BO 54 (56, 58, 60, 62, 62, 64, 64) sts for Back Neck, K 26 (28, 29, 30, 31, 31, 30, 31) sts for Left Back Shoulder.

Left Back Shoulder

Next Row (WS): Work across row.
Next Row (RS): BO all sts.

Right Back Shoulder

Join new yarn, ready to work WS row.
Next Row (WS): Work across row.
Next Row (RS): BO all sts.

Armhole Shaping/Right Front

Replace held Right Front sts on the needle. With WS facing, join new yarn. Continue working Right Front V-neck shaping on RS

rows, and begin working Armhole shaping at the armhole edge on WS rows, using Sloped Bind Off for all shaping.
BO 2 (2, 2, 2, 3, 2, 2, 3) sts every WS row 1 time, then BO 2 sts every WS row, 0 (0, 1, 1, 1, 1, 2, 2) time(s); then BO 1 st every WS row, 3 (3, 3, 4, 5, 6, 8, 9) times.

Continue working even at the armhole edge, and bind off as described in the V-Neck Shaping/Right Front section.

Sleeve (Make 2)

Sleeves are worked flat from the wrist up. Follow Sleeve chart, reading from the bottom up, RS (odd numbered) rows from right to left, and WS (even numbered) rows from left to right. Refer to special instructions for M1R/M1L: Sleeve Increases.

Sleeve Cuff

With MC and the Cable cast on method, CO 58 (60, 62, 64, 66, 68, 70, 72) sts.

Work rows 1-16 of Sleeve Chart in Corrugated Rib pattern (over an even number of sts).
With MC only, work next two chart rows as set up rows:
Row 17 (RS): Knit.
Row 18 (WS): Purl.
Begin working in Stranded Fair Isle pattern, continue following Sleeve chart, working first and last st of each row as K1 for a neat selvedge.

Inc Row (RS): K1, M1R, K in pattern to last two sts, M1L, K1. 2 sts increased.
Repeat Inc row on every 8th (8th, 8th, 8th, 6th, 6th, 6th, 8th) row, 12 (8, 4, 3, 22, 19, 24, 2) times, and then on every 6th (6th, 6th, 6th, 4th, 4th, 4th, 6th) row, 8 (13, 18, 19, 1, 5, 1, 22) times. 98 (102, 106, 108, 112, 116, 120, 120) sts on needle.

Work even until sleeve measures 21 (20.75, 20.5, 20.25, 20, 19.75, 21.5, 21.5)" from cast on edge, ending on a WS row.

Sleeve Cap Shaping

Sleeve cap shaping occurs at the beginning of RS and WS rows, using Sloped Bind Off.
Beg with RS facing, working bind offs at beg of each RS and WS row:
BO 4 (4, 4, 4, 4, 7, 7, 7) sts on every row; then BO 2 (2, 2, 2, 3, 2, 2, 3) sts on every row; then BO 2 sts on every row, 0 (0, 1, 1, 1, 1, 2, 2) time(s); then BO 1 st on every row, 3 (3, 3, 4, 5, 6, 8, 9) times, ending on a WS row.

Next Row (RS): BO all rem 80 (84, 84, 84, 84, 82, 78, 74) sts.
Sleeve length measures 22.25 (22, 22, 22, 22, 22, 24.5, 24.75)" from cast on edge.

Belt

Worked flat, in Corrugated Rib pattern over odd number of stitches, and from bottom hem up to top hem. When changing contrast colors C2, C3, and C4, cut yarn leaving approx a 5" tail for later weaving in across same color rows on WS. MC and C1 are carried at side edge on WS of Belt.

Hem

With MC, and Cable cast on, CO 15 sts. Work chart Rows 1 and 2 in Corrugated Rib over an odd number of sts:
Row 1 (RS): *K1, P1, rep from * to last st, K1.
Row 2 (WS): *P1, K1, rep from * to last st, P1.
Repeat rows 3-14 of Belt Chart as established, until Belt length measures 69.75 (73.75, 77.75, 81.75, 85.75, 89.75, 93.75, 97.75)" from cast edge, ending on a WS row.

Work Hem Rib Rows 1-2 in MC as follows:
Hem Rib Row 1 (RS): *K1, P1, rep from * to last st, K1.
Hem Rib Row 2 (WS): *P1, K1, rep from * to last st, P1.

Next Row (RS): BO all sts.
Belt measures 70 (74, 78, 82, 86, 90, 94, 98)" from cast on edge.

Finishing

Weave in ends. Prior to seaming, pin according to Garment Schematic and thoroughly spray wet to block. Sew Right Front Shoulder to Right Back Shoulder, and then Left Front Shoulder to Left Back Shoulder. *Place marker at center of each Sleeve Cap, and at center of each Shoulder seam. Beginning with Right Sleeve Cap, match markers and sew Right Sleeve Cap, easing into armhole. Sew Right Sleeve seam. * Rep from * to * changing instructions for Left Sleeve. Weave in Belt ends, working each individual yarn tail across entire same color row. Begin working Front/Neck Band.

Front/Neck Band

Note: When picking up sts at Right and Left Fronts, *PU 1 st for every row. At Right and Left V-Necks, PU 1 st every slanted/curved row, and PU 1 st every other row at straight rows. At Back Neck, PU 1 st for every stitch, plus one extra st (rib balance stitch). Odd number of sts required for Front/Neck Band.

Beg with RS facing and MC, start at cast on edge of Right Front (at hem), PU & knit 128 (128, 128, 128, 128, 128, 144, 144) sts, then PU & knit 92 sts at Right Front V-neck, continue to Back Neck, PU & knit 27 (28, 29, 30, 31, 31, 32, 32) sts (half Back Neck). Using spare needle, continue picking up sts for Back Neck, PU & knit 28 (29, 30, 31, 32, 32, 33, 33), then PU & knit 92 sts at Left Front V-neck, and then cont to Left Front, PU 128 (128, 128, 128, 128, 128, 144, 144) sts. 495 (497, 499, 501, 503, 503, 537, 537) sts on needle.

Work rows 2-16 of Front/Neck Band Chart in Corrugated Rib pattern (over an odd number of sts).

Loosely BO all sts.

Weave in any remaining ends. Re-block finished garment according to Garment Schematic, pinning Right Front/Neck Band overlapping Left Front/Neck Band. Sew "male" snap to inside (WS) Left Front at corner where Left Front and V-neck meet, and along seam created by picking up stitches. Sew "female" snap on front (RS) of Left Front, to correspond with placement of male snap. Repeat for second snap, placing 1.5" below previous snap.

Back

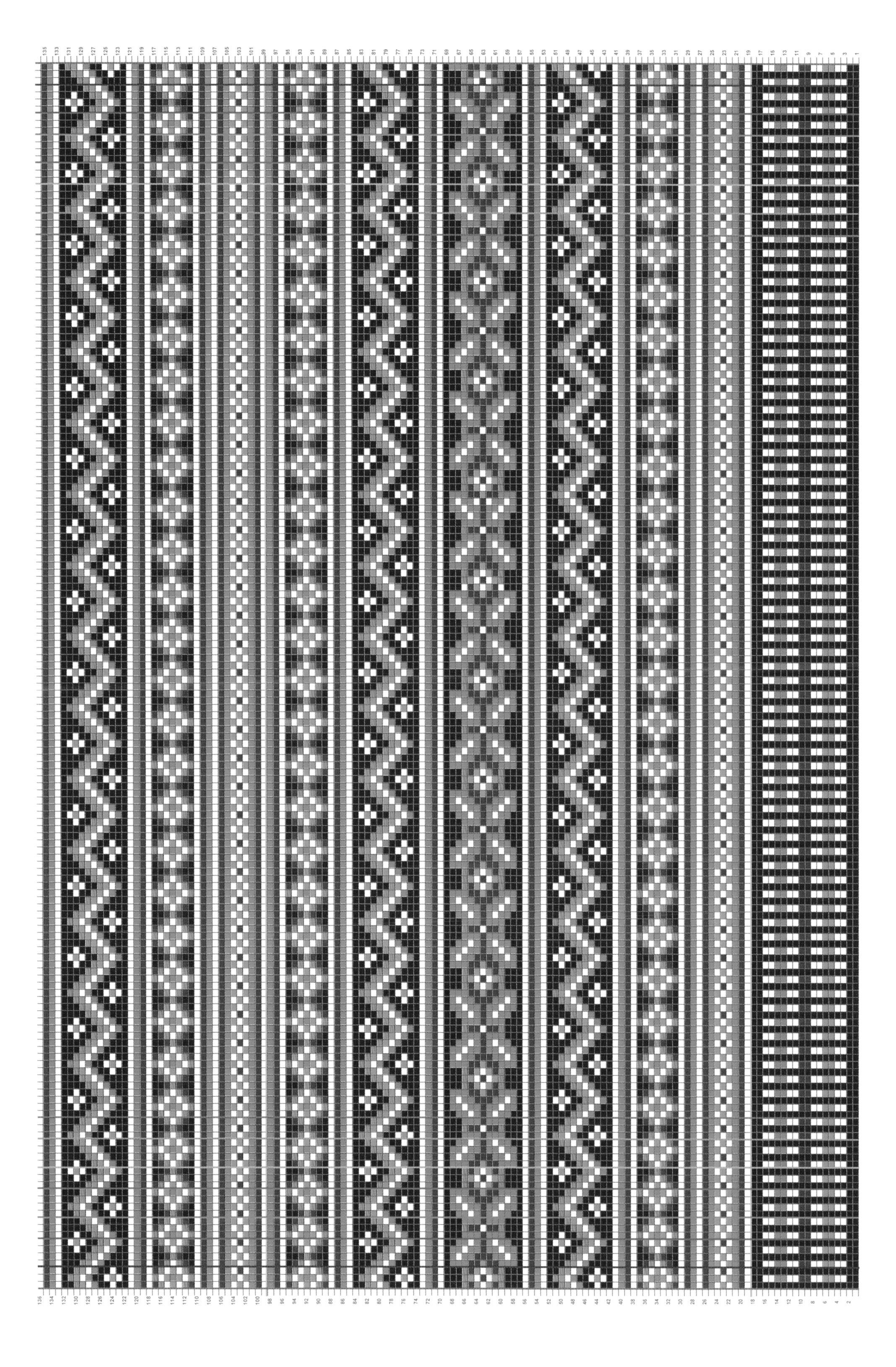

Left Front

Right Front

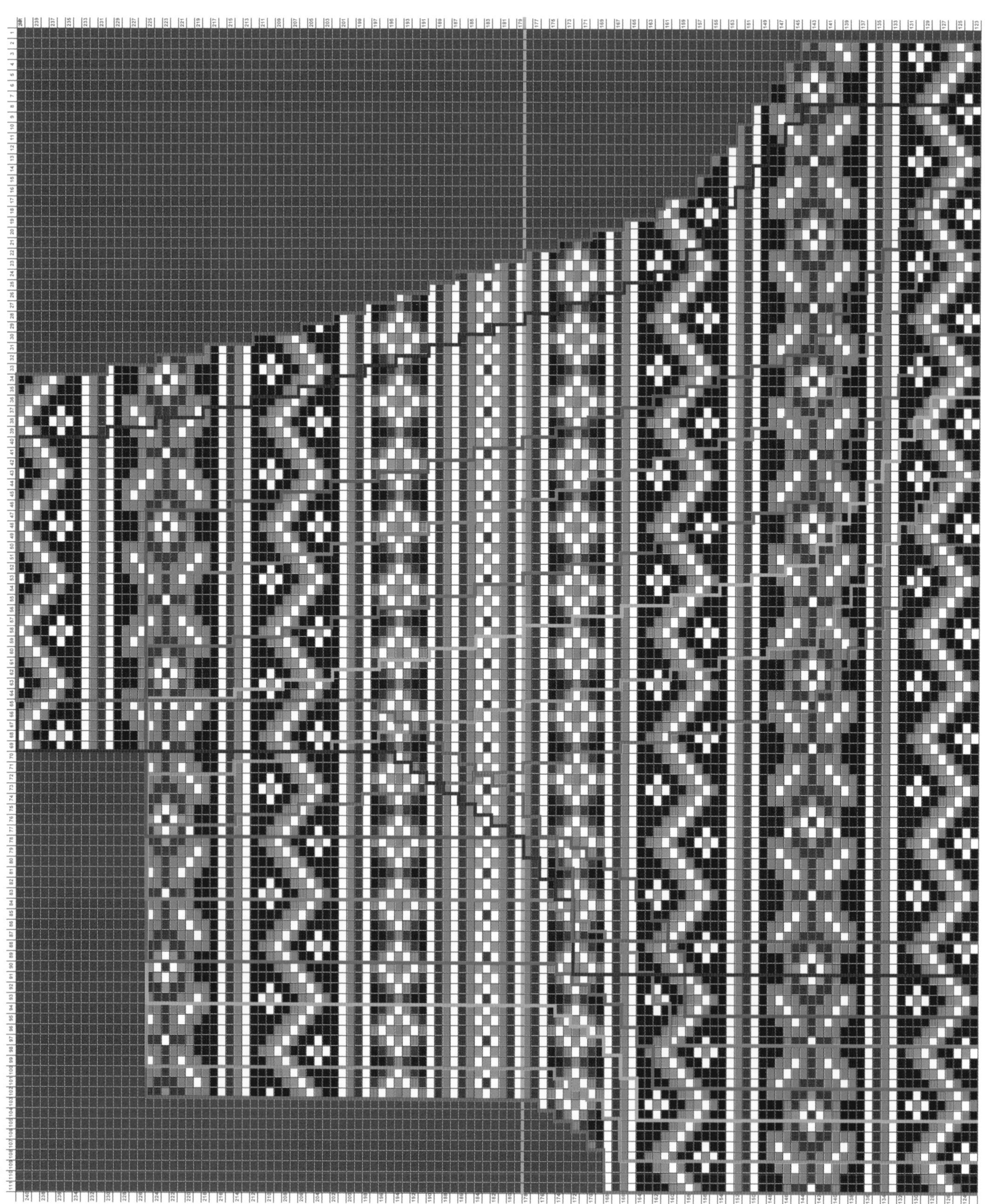

Sleeve

Pattern Repeat 1

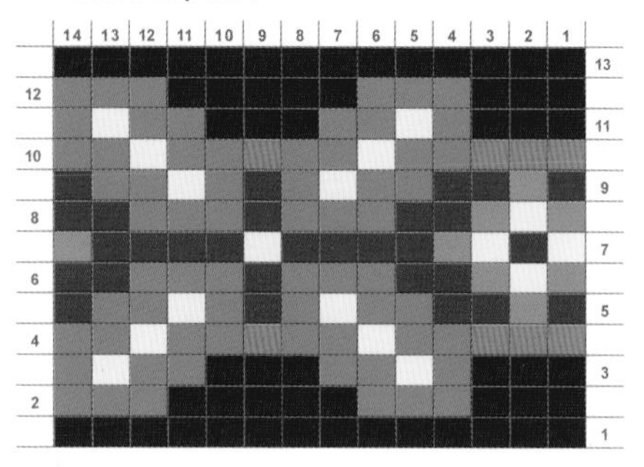

Pattern Repeat 2

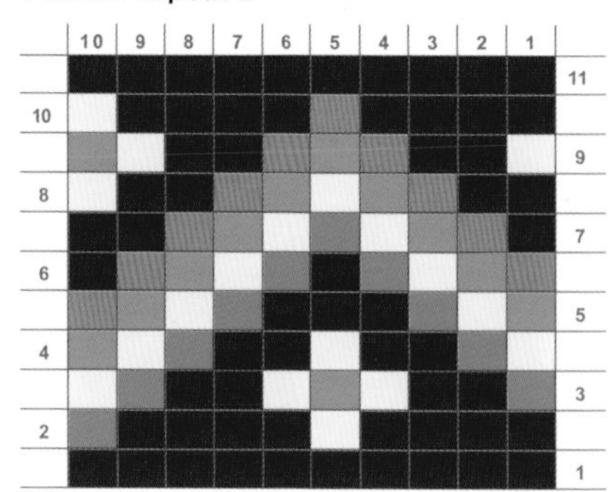

Pattern Repeat 3

Pattern Repeat 4

Pattern Repeat 5

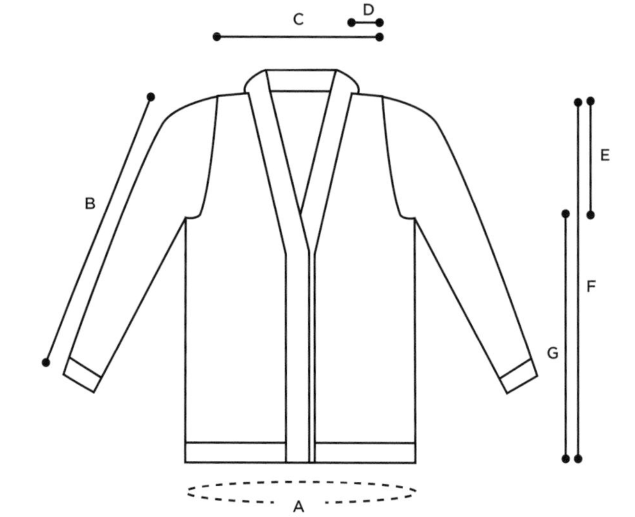

Front Neck Band

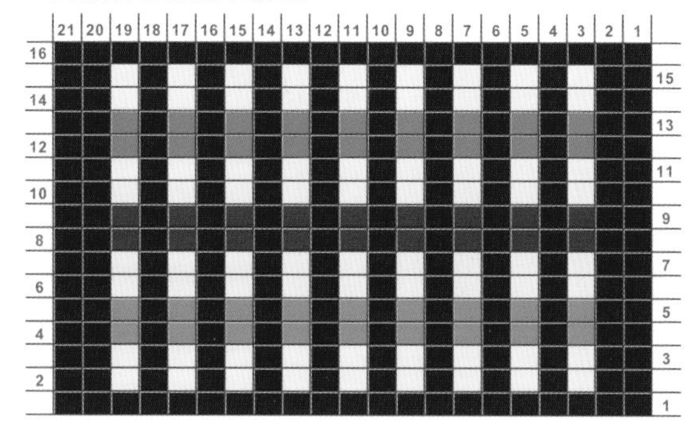

A 37.5 (39.25, 41.5, 43.25, 45.5, 47.25, 49.5, 51.25)"
B 22.25 (22, 22, 22, 22, 22, 24.5, 24.75)"
C 15 (16, 16.5, 17, 17.75, 17.75, 17.75, 18)"
D 3.75 (4, 4, 4.25, 4.5, 4.5, 4.25, 4.5)"
E 7 (7.25, 7.5, 7.75, 8, 8.25, 8.5, 8.5)"
F 28 (28, 28, 28, 28, 28, 30, 30)"
G 21 (20.75, 20.5, 20.25, 20, 19.75, 21.5, 21.5)"

Belt

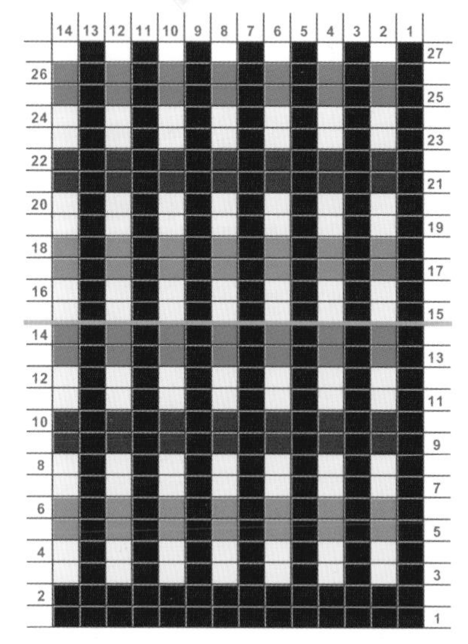

Legend

- RS: Knit / WS: Purl
- Placeholder: no stitch
- MC
- C1
- C2
- C3
- C4
- C5

- size 37.5"
- size 39.25
- size 41.5"
- size 43.25"
- size 45.5"
- size 47.25"
- size 49.5"
- size 51.25"
- pattern repeat

Knit Picks yarn is both luxe and affordable—a seeming contradiction trounced! But it's not just about the pretty colors; we also care deeply about fiber quality and fair labor practices, leaving you with a gorgeously reliable product you'll turn to time and time again.

THIS COLLECTION FEATURES

Palette
Fingering Weight
100% Peruvian Highland Wool

Wool of the Andes Worsted
Worsted Weight
100% Peruvian Highland Wool

Wool of the Andes Sport
Sport Weight
100% Peruvian Highland Wool

View these beautiful yarns and more at www.KnitPicks.com

Abbreviations

Abbreviation	Meaning
BO	bind off
cn	cable needle
CC	contrast color
CDD	Centered double dec
CO	cast on
cont	continue
dec	decrease(es)
DPN(s)	double pointed needle(s)
EOR	every other row
inc	increase
K	knit
K2tog	knit two sts together
KFB	knit into the front and back of stitch
K-wise	knitwise
LH	left hand
M	marker
M1	make one stitch
M1L	make one left-leaning stitch
M1R	make one right-leaning stitch
MC	main color
P	purl
P2tog	purl 2 sts together
PM	place marker
PFB	purl into the front and back of stitch
PSSO	pass slipped stitch over
PU	pick up
P-wise	purlwise
rep	repeat
Rev St st	reverse stockinette stitch
RH	right hand
rnd(s)	round(s)
RS	right side
Sk	skip
Sk2p	sl 1, k2tog, pass slipped stitch over k2tog: 2 sts dec
SKP	sl, k, psso: 1 st dec
SL	slip
SM	slip marker
SSK	sl, sl, k these 2 sts tog
SSP	sl, sl, p these 2 sts tog tbl
SSSK	sl, sl, sl, k these 3 sts tog
St st	stockinette stitch
sts	stitch(es)
TBL	through back loop
TFL	through front loop
tog	together
W&T	wrap & turn (see specific instructions in pattern)
WE	work even
WS	wrong side
WYIB	with yarn in back
WYIF	with yarn in front
YO	yarn over